I0625323

Odyssey into the Night

Guidance for Spirited Women
Daring to Change

C. Loran Hills

Edgewood Publishing Company

Edgewood Publishing Company

47 Upper Road

Sheridan, Wyoming 82801

Ordering Information:

Quantity sales. Special discounts are available on quantity purchases by corporations, associations, and others. For details, contact the "Special Sales Department" at the address above.

Odyssey into the Night/ C. Loran Hills. —1st ed.

ISBN 979-8-218-16831-5

Monarch of Heart, Depth, and Focus
Explorer of Sacred Realms
Queen of Wanderlust

I am a sparkling dewdrop on a leaf
The song of a meadowlark
An unruly fury
A mighty force
Shapeshifting on the night wind
Reckless and untamed
Wilderness breathes me

For Alyson and Amber, with all my love

Odyssey into the Night

TABLE OF CONTENTS

INTRODUCTIONS

JOURNALS, CHANGE, AND AGING

MUSINGS AND MYSTERIES

ILLUMINATING SPIRITUAL PRACTICE

FINAL THOUGHTS

BIBLIOGRAPHY

ACKNOWLEDGMENTS

INTRODUCTIONS

Odyssey into the Night

A LITTLE BIT ABOUT ME

My story is one of suffering transmuted by grace into one of growth and occasional transcendence. I've learned that my experience, strength and hope may be of benefit to others. My path of personal and spiritual growth is what has sustained me.

Life, like my stories, is not linear. It moves in a spiral pattern through rotations around the sun, seasons, lunar cycles. Growth is sometimes two steps forward and one step back, with a little side-to-side or upside-down for good measure. It's about progress, not perfection.

My hope is that something I've written or learned may help someone else. We all arrive on the planet with a deck of playing cards. The decks aren't always stacked the same; however, we all breathe oxygen, drink water, bleed, laugh and cry, love and sometimes hate. We all want to be happy.

For as long as I can remember, I've wondered about life, the meaning of life, and why we're here. I'm not sure there are answers but I do know that we are interconnected with everything and everyone. We live on a small blue ball in the middle of a vast, incomprehensible universe.

I think we need to get our collective shit together. I work on my own issues. I'd like everyone else to work on theirs. If we could all do this, take responsibility for ourselves, pay attention to the needs of others, practice compassion, and start giving back to Earth, we might have a chance of surviving. Otherwise, there's the probability of extinction.

If you're willing to open your heart and mind to new ways of looking at the world, you might find what I write about is helpful. My wish and motivation for compiling my thoughts, essays, memories, and musings is to spark your curiosity or some new thoughts about your own personal and spiritual growth.

What I've compiled here was written from 2011 to 2020. It's not necessarily in chronological order. There is a flow through my life, threads of thought woven throughout different stages. There may be some repetition.

There is a mistaken belief that once you have grown up (whatever that it is), it's time to stop growing as a person. It's not true. As we age, we might become more curious about who we are. Tools are available for diving into self-discovery. Unfortunately, our lives can become so hectic that it's difficult to focus on our interior landscapes, our secret gardens. On the other hand, you can't lose a sense of self if you never had one. Maybe it's time to discover who you really are.

I've been thinking about what I can do to bring more joy, peace, and healing to the world. It seems that when I open my heart to new possibilities, creative experiences increase. Art, music, spirituality, and love are the forces that inspire me.

A LITTLE BIT MORE ABOUT ME

I am a zealot for words.
An ardent believer in expression.
A fervent reader.
An enthusiastic supporter of ideas.
I am an ink slinger.

WHERE I'M FROM

I'm from colonialism and military honors
I'm from blissful ignorance born of privilege
I'm from servants holding silver trays of crystal
     glasses
I'm from a nanny I don't remember

I'm from a brick house surrounded by oak trees
I'm from piano lessons on a Steinway grand
I'm from Persian rugs and French antiques
I'm from college educations

I'm from a mysterious past linked by DNA to
     Ashkenazi Jews
I'm from secrets held

Note: Adapted from a template by George Ella Lyon's
"Where I'm From" poem.

MOONDAY MUSINGS #3

An answer to "Show us you" from Hannah Marcotti.

I am:

Christine Loran Hills
64
white
cis-gendered
able-bodied
heteronormal
well educated
a woman of privilege
a daughter, wife, mother, sister, aunt, friend
a grassroots organizer
a retired therapist
a writer
a photographer
someone who thinks deeply
an inclusive, intersectional, expansive feminist (thank
you, Alicia Garza)
Wild Brazen Witchy Moon Amazon Buddhist Goddess
Woman (thank you, Kathryn)
a recovering alcoholic with 22+ years of sobriety
a part of nature
a TreeSister
dancing in the still point
shimmering radiance
spiraling transformation
vibrating subatomic particles

Who I am isn't really any of these labels or behaviors. Who I am probably won't be remembered 100 years from now. I'm impermanent like everyone else. I believe that it's important to do the right thing, be as loving as I can be, and to cause as little harm as possible.

Note: Twenty Moonday Musings were posted on Loran Hills' Facebook Author Page in 2017.

Monday was originally coined as Moonday by the Greeks and Romans. (Wikipedia)

TURTLES ARE UNDER-RATED

Turtle mythology is ancient. They are known to help unite heaven and earth within your own life. Those of us in the United States live on Turtle Island. (Andrews, 2011)

For me, turtles represent taking time to allow things to flow naturally. I'm not a high-energy person. I'm not a racehorse. Connecting heaven and earth keeps me spiritually healthy. Sometimes I need to retreat into a shell to work things out. Sometimes I need to grow roots and get centered because if my head is in the stars for too long I get out of balance.

For a long time, I felt shame about being a little slow and a little less energetic than my friends. Now, I'm growing into my turtle nature and learning to accept it. I can control my own pace. If I try to deny my true nature I end up stressed out and unhappy.

My Voice is deep inside me. It's been slowly emerging over time since I was a child and could not speak my Truth. There was a time I raged about my Truth but that was not from a state of clarity. I am actually old enough now to voice the Truth that I could not speak then.

turtle girl

one restless night
she woke
thirsty
itchy

wings grew out of her shoulders

silly girl she thought
turtles don't have wings

oh yes they do

when the moon is full
she flies away

remembering desire
she swims in the sea of opportunity

AN AUTUMN WOMAN IN SPRING (2018)

Where do I begin?

Start at the beginning? I don't want to.

Start where you are. Except that, if I start where I am here today by the time you, the reader, see this, I will be farther into the future.

Start future writing? I'm reading the book I wrote and thinking it's quite an accomplishment!

Time appears to be on a continuum made of a straight line, but that line is an illusion. Life itself is illusory. We're masses of cosmic molecules moving around interacting with other molecules.

Contemplation? It's possible to think too much.

I want to write about interconnectedness. Thicht Nhat Hanh, a renowned Buddhist monk, says that we Inter-Are. This is how it works: I'm sitting on a couch that was made in a factory somewhere. It's covered with an orange synthetic fabric that was most likely made somewhere else. My feet are on a floor covered by a carpet made by different people than the ones who made my shoes. I'm sitting in a building made of materials created from all over the world.

As I look outside the window, I can see trees blooming - there's a glorious profusion of white blossoms, the first I've seen this spring. I sat here for an hour on my computer, a MacBook that was designed in Cupertino, California but manufactured in Suzhou, China, on this couch made by someone, and never noticed the blossoms until now. The wind is blowing the trees but the blossoms are new enough that the petals aren't falling to the ground yet.

Who grew the trees? Who planted the trees? Who waters them? How much water and sun do they require in the courtyard to survive? Are there enough nutrients in the ground for them to stay healthy?

See? Take one item and try to trace it back to its origin. It's hard to do. So, how can I trace myself back to my origins? Do I start with my ancestors who did actually come over on the Mayflower? Or, do I begin with my parents and how they met?

I begin here.

Odyssey into the Night

JOURNALS, CHANGE, AND AGING

Odyssey into the Night

22

WHY KEEP JOURNALS IF YOU MIGHT BURN THEM
(2018)

I started keeping a diary when I was eight years old. I complained about my younger sister a lot. I kept another journal in high school filled with unrequited longings. There are numerous embarrassing passages.

In my early twenties, I discovered Anaïs Nin and her Diaries. I bought and read the entire set of six volumes. She was French, she hung out with artists and writers in Paris and Harlem. She traveled to Bali, inspiring me to go, too. She wrote about dreams, her psychoanalysis, her desire to create a language for women. She wrangled with abandonment issues after her father left her family when she was twelve. I learned a lot from her, about life and about keeping a diary.

Inspired to journal with meaning and depth, I used Ira Progoff's methods from his book, *At a Journal Workshop.* I maintained volumes of information about my life's Steppingstones. I wrote endless dialogues with my body and kept track of the calories I consumed when dieting. I filled sections with inspirational quotes and inebriated ramblings. Eventually, I tired of Progroff's complicated approach.

I experimented for years with different methods. Occasionally I would review my journals and leave myself notes in present time; such as, "I can't believe I knew this then," or "Why am I writing about the same things over and over?" I recorded memories I never wanted my daughters to read. Ever.

The decision to burn my journals might have solidified when I read an entire volume filled with miserable rantings over a doomed relationship. It was full of endless recriminations and self-loathing. I couldn't bear to read it. I was afraid I might die with all these words available for someone else to read.

One hot day in summer I took a torch to a huge pile of notebooks and papers. Some volumes took a long time to burn as I watched words disappear in smoke. Part of me wanted to reach in and rescue the journals. The other part felt relief. When it was all nothing but ash, I felt lighter.

Occasionally I regret that I can't look something up, that I have to depend on my faulty memory of the past. I also didn't burn everything nor did I stop writing. I'm compelled to continue my journey of self-reflection. Journaling helps me clarify ideas, thoughts and feelings. There are things I can't figure out unless I'm writing with pen to paper. I have a nature journal, art journals, sketchbooks and writing journals.

Six years ago I wrote a piece for Tiny Buddha, <u>10 Journaling Tips to Help You Heal, Grow and Thrive.</u> For a while, I was the #1 hit on Google for journaling, my 15 minutes of fame. I think journaling is important. Some people refuse to keep a journal because they are afraid someone else will read it. A lock box solves that problem. It's possible to keep a private journal online, if you believe anything on the internet is truly private. Or, write as openly and honestly as possible, then burn it. Don't worry about spelling, grammar or punctuation.

Either you like to write or you don't. It's a useful tool. If you feel anxious or your life feels miserable, I recommend developing a practice of self-reflection. There are many methods available for peering inside our brains, examining our neural pathways, and creating healthier ones. I'm grateful that through hard work and maturation, at last, I have insight and even a little wisdom.

This essay originally appeared on Medium.com.

10 JOURNALING TIPS TO HELP YOU GROW AND THRIVE

Keeping a journal has many positive benefits. Journaling can help with personal growth and development. By regularly recording your thoughts you will gain insight into your behaviors and moods. Journaling can be used for problem-solving and stress reduction. It's been proven to improve mental and physical health. It can lead to increased self-esteem.

Anxiety disorders, mood disorders, and substance abuse can be treated with a combination of medication and counseling. In addition, writing in a journal is an effective tool for use in the healing process.

I started keeping a diary at age 8. As I grew up, I wrote the normal kinds of teen angst entries but eventually, I turned journaling into a more sophisticated practice. In my 20's I was inspired by reading all of Anais Nin's Diaries.

I studied Ira Progoff's *At a Journal Workshop* and implemented his methods—an elaborate design for generating the energy for change. Using his methods I was able to sort through turbulent emotions during the divorce from my first husband and discover hidden lessons from the experience.

To this day I continue to use some of his techniques as well as others I've learned. Recently I've discovered a new creative world in art journaling. Using mixed media has helped me express myself in refreshing and unusual ways.

There is a lot of power in the written word but occasionally words are hard to find. By drawing or making a collage I have been able to create a representation of how I feel that moves beyond my analytical writing.

Writing has helped me to process not only failed relationships but also to recover from grief and loss. Reading back through my journals has helped me reflect on where I used to be and where I am now in my life. It's a method of allowing the light of understanding and compassion to shine on my past. In *The Artist's Way*, Julia Cameron suggests writing three handwritten pages or 750 words every morning. At first, there is a lot of "dumping" but eventually little jewels of wisdom and direction emerge. I found myself creatively energized when I participated with a group for 12 weeks using her book as a guide.
If you want to improve your perspective on life and clarify issues, start writing in a journal.

You can't know where you're going if you don't know where you are.

Be sure your journal will remain private or write online so that you are writing for your eyes only.

Here are 10 tips to get started:

1. Start writing about where you are in your life at this moment.

Describe your living situation, your work, and your relationships. Are you right where you want to be?

2. For five to ten minutes just start writing in a "stream of consciousness."

Don't edit your thoughts or feelings and don't correct your grammar. Don't censor your thoughts.

3. Start a dialogue with your inner child by writing in your subdominant hand.

Answer with your dominant hand. What issues emerge?

4. Cultivate an attitude of gratitude by maintaining a daily list of things you appreciate, including uplifting quotes.

Keep it in one journal or in a separate section so that you can read through it all at once. When you feel down you can read through it for a boost of gratitude and happiness.

5. Start a journal of self-portraits.

You can take pictures, draw colors or shapes or collage images. Learn to love and accept yourself just the way you are today.

6. Keep a nature diary to connect with the natural world.

The world we live in is a magical and mysterious place. Record the things you notice about the sky, the weather, and the seasons.

7. Maintain a log of successes.

Begin by writing the big ones you remember then regularly jot down small successes that occur during the week. As you pay attention, your list will grow and inspire you.

8. Keep a log or playlist of your favorite songs.

Write about the moods they evoke. When you hear a song that triggers a strong memory, write down how you feel and explore that time and space of your life.

9. If there's something you are struggling with or an event that's disturbing you, write about it in the third person.

This will give you distance and provide a new perspective. Write down what you learned about yourself.

10. Develop your intuition.

Write down questions or concerns then take a deep breath and listen for a response from your Higher Self. Let yourself write automatically. If you don't get an answer right away, look for signs during the day. We all have dark days, black moods, and anxious feelings. Use writing in a journal to explore the darkness. You will find your inner light when you do.

Originally posted on TinyBuddha.com.

WHAT IS THE HEART OF THE MATTER? (2013)

**You are the center from which your life flows
in ever-changing cycles.**

Where is your center? What's in there?

Are you holding on to misery? Tightly grasping, rigidly clinging? Desperately reaching for something to soothe the pain?

Perhaps it feels familiar and oddly comfortable. You know this drill. Continue the pattern and what do you get?

Constriction. Depression. Anxiety. Despair. You tell yourself, "It's always been this way. I've always been this way. It's no use trying to change."

Do you believe in change? Whether you do or not, change is inevitable. Nothing lasts.

Does this thought cause you fear? Do you try to cling even harder? What happens when you squeeze tighter?

You can't breathe. You can't think. You cry or yell or scream.

What happens when you let go and loosen your grip? Is there space to breathe? Is there a feeling of openness?

Can you stand on the edge of a cliff and look down? Can you leap empty-handed? Can you fly?

What happens when there is no depression? No anxiety? No despair?

It feels really weird at first. Is that bad? Does it feel terrible? Or, maybe, it's a little bit exciting? Or even exhilarating?

Can you feel something stirring or shifting? In the spring there is a new, raw energy that creates life.

Is the flower bud that opens up into full bloom afraid? Of course not!

What is there to fear? To lose bitterness, resentment, or anger is to allow love, forgiveness, joy, grace, and healing light to enter the wounded places.

My center is a lodestar. My guiding star is the calling to rouse, awaken, inspire, and incite others to action.

The heart of the matter is that I am compelled, driven to continue diving below the surface and to keep soaring into the sky.

I look at all angles. I allow myself to feel.

I was not allowed to feel for a long time. Then I numbed the feelings. I am not numb now.

Feelings make me vulnerable and that creates fear but it's better than anger or mean behavior.

I seesaw up and down, happy, sad, joyful, depressed, gleeful, raging.

Where is the center? It's in me. I am the fulcrum of change. I am the axis.

I'm restoring the power within that grows, that lights the way, that provides solace in tough times.

Embody the sacred.

Stand on the ground and look up. Connect to the earth and the sky. Let love drench you like a warm, soft, cleansing rain.

You'll be glad you did.

Remember we live on a small blue planet suspended in space. We forget that we are made of swirling molecules. We are fragile. We are here today and gone tomorrow.

Decide what matters. And then do it one step at a time.

13 WAYS TO COPE WITH CHANGE

When my first love died suddenly, my life changed dramatically and permanently. Barely twenty-two at the time, I had no coping skills and no support system. I couldn't anticipate how deep sorrow would render me completely devastated and heartbroken.

As a result, I engaged in extremely self-destructive behavior. I believed I was going "with the flow," but in truth, I did so many reckless things that I'm surprised I survived. I didn't know how to deal with my anguish in any other way.

Because life was obviously unpredictable, I decided to stop making plans. I didn't know what it meant to be responsible for my choices or how to be emotionally healthy. Many years were spent in a foggy haze of grief, depression, and anger.

Slowly, over time, I turned my life around. I engaged in therapy, recovery work, and spiritual exploration. I studied everything I could on personal growth. I learned to identify and express my feelings appropriately.

Ultimately, I decided to make plans again, with the intimate knowledge that things could always change in the blink of an eye.

Of course, there will always be events that are out of my control, but at the same time, I can choose my reaction. Now, I actively seek ways to maintain my peace of mind and serenity.

I've learned to accept that change is a part of life and a process that cannot be avoided. Some changes are easier to accept than others, but the decisions about how to cope with those changes are mine.

To change is to transform, alter, modify or shift; these are behaviors that I've integrated into my life in order to survive emotionally.

Growth requires action. Think of a seed. The potential to grow is there, but nothing happens until that seed is planted and watered.

My desire to grow arose from recognizing the difference between where I was and where I wanted to be. Internal changes came from an aspiration within for things to be different and a desire to cultivate new behaviors. I chose to transform the dark and tangled garden of my life.

Internal change requires a distinct set of skills. These skills are not difficult to learn but do require a shift in thinking and behavior.

Here are thirteen suggestions for managing the ebb and flow of changes around you.

1. Recognize that change is part of the fabric of our lives.

Just as the seasons change, so do we. Some changes we can choose, others we do not.

2. Clear your mind.

Develop awareness of the changes that occur around you. Notice the natural changes that take place in everyday life.

3. Establish a quality of purpose, a goal, or some objective to be reached.

Start small. Practice making minor changes to build confidence.

4. Imagine the elation of manifesting your intentions.

Visualize what you want to create in as much detail as possible, then release it. Allow change to flow naturally without force.

5. Trust your intuition.

There is a deep well of inner wisdom within you. This innate sense of wisdom will guide you.

6. Identify your fears about change, whether it is the fear of failure or the fear of success.

Perhaps it's the fear of not doing anything or the fear of doing something new that prevents you from changing. In any case, you deserve to be successful.

7. Remember that change requires courage.

It is the ability to act in spite of feeling insecure or uncertain. Ask for support and allow yourself to receive it.

8. Take a loving and gentle approach.

Don't beat yourself up if you don't succeed instantly. Change requires consistency and persistent action.

9. Be curious.

Try experimenting with new foods, listening to new music, varying your route to work, or shopping at a different store. Question whether or not you are acting out of habit and investigate new behaviors.

10. Expect to feel uncomfortable with what's unfamiliar.

Anticipate resistance. Give yourself permission to feel weird.

11. Consider healing activities that will enhance your senses of sight, sound, smell, taste, and touch.

Make a list of things you like to do to relax. Take a walk, write in your journal, or drink a cup of tea.

12. Listen to your self-talk.

The words you say to yourself need to come from your heart, where wisdom and compassion live. Say all the things you want and need to hear.

13. Create incentives and rewards for changing.

Evaluate what motivates you. Generate enthusiasm by celebrating along the way.

You will discover that you have strength you don't know you possess until you need it. Cultivate your

skills so that when you do need to cope with a major change, you will be able to stay as emotionally healthy as possible. You'll be relieved that you created good habits for managing change.
May joy fill your days. May you be happy.

This essay originally appeared In TinyBuddha.com.

OPEN THE DOOR TO CREATIVITY (2017)

The empty page. A blank canvas. Knitting needles and a ball of yarn. Fabric and thread. New creations emerge from our imagination.

When I rediscovered my creativity in 2010, I wanted to bathe in color, pour paint all over my body, and roll around in it. The doors to my creative expression opened through art journaling, writing, and photography.

Nature is inherently creative. The earth, dark and fecund, is fertile ground. A small seed contains a blueprint within its totality. That seed grows into a plant with help from rain and sun, the elements support its growth. The plant blooms and bears fruit for the harvest. So it is with a creative idea. It begins in the imagination, finds fertile ground, grows with love and attention, then blooms into something lovely, delightful, or engaging.

Unfortunately, there are many blocks to creative expression. Energy, time, and money are in short supply when it comes to creative pursuits. Women are too busy meeting everyone else's needs to prioritize their own needs or desires for creative projects.

In school, traditional education can force us into conformity. If a student creates something for a grade based on the teacher's opinion, then their authentic voice gets lost in the creative process. At its worst, school can destroy creative self-confidence. One unkind or cruel statement can stop someone in their tracks, never to try again. The fear of critical judgment can lead to a lifetime of fear from trying anything called art.

My privileged life growing up was steeped in art and music. As a child, my parents took me to symphonies and museums. I studied classical piano. I majored in Art History in college. I was trained to look at art with a critical eye and learned about light and composition. These skills help me with my photography even though I have no formal education in photography.

The art classes I took were a different story. I didn't conform to the professors' expectations and argued regularly about theory. My experiences with them led me to believe that I didn't have talent. It wasn't true but I believed it for a long time.

We are individuals with different perspectives, ideas, needs, experiences. We are unique in our perceptions. Two people can witness the same event and yet describe it in completely different ways. So, in order to freely express ourselves, we need encouragement to overcome the negative inner critic, engage in imaginative play and let go of fear.

In Unraveled: an exercise in untangling, Staci Jordan Shelton points out that creativity is a valuable form of self-care. As much as I love creative processes, I never looked at it quite this way before. It's a way of listening to our intuition and expressing ourselves in our own unique way. Another perk of creativity is that we build a more meaningful and healthy life. Creative projects help us lift our hearts and expand our spirits, especially if we practice with love, acceptance, and compassion toward our efforts.

You can begin at any age, just begin. Don't let past critical comments or judgments stop you. Start by carving out a little time during the week for creative activity. Take a community ed class. Make pottery, keep a nature journal, dance, write poetry, participate in community theater, volunteer in an art museum, attend free cultural events. It's not ever too late to live more art-fully. It feeds your spirit and improves your mental health.

Get started today. There's no time like the present. Try something new. It doesn't have to be perfect or even beautiful. It only needs to be an honest expression of something meaningful to you. You'll feel better when you do.

stacijordanshelton.podia.com

50 YEARS AGO SEEMS IMPOSSIBLE (2020)

I can remember what it was like "before."

Did you know that the Environmental Protection Agency was created in December 1970? This year we will celebrate the fiftieth anniversary of Earth Day. Can you imagine a time when there wasn't a global environmental movement?

I can't help but look back even though I hardly believe it's possible to be this old. (I am not, however, elderly.) I remember sooty window sills in our New York apartment and how dirty the Potomac River was in Washington, D.C. I also remember a lot of other things in light of what didn't exist then.

Fifty years ago I was a junior in high school. I read books before bedtime. There were no Kindles or Nooks.

I set my electric alarm clock for school. It was placed on my desk away from my bed. I wouldn't wake up without getting up to turn it off in the morning. Sometimes I could get up, turn it off and go back to bed without ever waking up. Once I was awake for sure, I'd go to my sister's room, flick the lights on and off a couple of times and yell, "Time to get up!" She appreciated it.

Long straight hair was my dream but my hair was curly. There were no straighteners or hair products. I slept on giant curlers to smooth out my hair. Sometimes I yanked the curlers out in my sleep because they were extremely uncomfortable.

Our mother didn't like to get up with us. On the rare mornings she felt guilty enough to fix us breakfast, she made us late for the bus. Usually, I drank chocolate Instant Breakfast before walking to the corner to wait for the bus. Girls weren't allowed to wear pants! During winter I was always cold in pantyhose and skirts.

If I had to write a research paper, I went to the school library, looked in the card catalog for materials, and pulled them off the shelf. When I had a big pile of books, I checked them out at the desk. We signed cards that came out of the back of the book and gave them to the librarian. There was no Wikipedia. There were no word processors for writing papers. Computers were cumbersome beasts run by piles of cards covered in mysterious plus and minus codes.

School was a safe place. We never had an active shooter drill. But girls couldn't play sports, there was no Title IX for women. Women weren't allowed to run marathons because their uterus might fall out.

Married women couldn't get financial credit without permission from their husbands. Consciousness-raising groups were just beginning as women shared their stories about domestic violence, rape and sexual abuse. There were no shelters.

If I wanted to talk to a friend, I called her on the phone. Our phone had push buttons and a long cord, creating a small measure of privacy out in the hall. We didn't have message machines. There was no texting, no social media. I don't have many pictures of me or my friends because there were no selfies. We didn't binge-watch anything. If we wanted to see a movie, we went to the theater. If we didn't know how to get there, we asked for directions or used a map because there was no GPS.

There was a choice of three stations on the TV and no remote control. We had to get up to change those channels. The Viet Nam war was raging. Every day there was a body count of American casualties along with footage of the fighting. War was real and present in everyone's living room. News reports were unsanitized.

There were no microwave ovens. Frozen meat had to be taken out to defrost for dinner. When we brought home groceries, it was all in paper bags. There wasn't fast food other than McDonald's which was a treat, not a staple.

Cars started with a key in the ignition. Gas was 36 cents a gallon. You were cool if you had an 8 track player for music. There was no streaming music. My dad had a Pontiac LeMans that was really fun to drive. Rehobeth Beach, Delaware was a three-hour drive from our house, if he drove. I made it there on my own in a little over two hours hauling ass on flat, straight roads. No fear of accidents, just exhilaration and a feeling of freedom.

Before all these things existed, I couldn't imagine what it would be like now. The Jetsons cartoon family talked on phones and could see the person calling. At the time it seemed impossible. Now I can FaceTime or Zoom with friends and family anywhere in the world in real-time. It never fails to amaze me. My computer, smartphone, Netflix and Hulu subscriptions are things I appreciate now. I drive a hybrid car. I like throwing something into the microwave to make dinner.

While writing for Medium.com, I can stop and look something up on Google (like the price of gasoline in 1970) and it's right at my fingertips. I don't have to wait to drive to the library when it opens on Monday morning.

I don't think 24-hour news cycles are a good thing. There's too much blathering. News ought not be entertainment but it is now. I don't care about the Kardashians or Ben Affleck's latest romance. I don't want to listen to endless speculation about events when there are no facts. Facts seem like a remote part of the past.

Fifty years ago we were warned about the climate heating up and ice caps melting. Despite of some progress, we aren't moving fast enough to mitigate all the effects of our consumer culture. My hair lights on fire when I consider the damage being done daily to people, animals and the environment.

And yet, in spite of it all, I'm still here. I come from a vanished place in time. Seeds were planted. We are reaping what we sowed. I can't imagine where we'll be in another fifty years. I hope we shift consciousness towards restoration of our planet. I won't live to see another fifty years but I want our youth to have a chance to grow old, too.

This essay originally appeared on Medium.com.

WHEN I WAS A BADASS (MAY 2017)

Sweat, blood and tears, that's what it took to gain rank in Tang Soo Do. My life was in turmoil. I was going through a divorce and a feminist rage stage. I was pissed off all the time about everything when I walked in to sign up for karate classes. Underneath it all, feelings of shame and inadequacy were welling up in me again.

I was terrified. PE was torture for me when I was a klutzy kid. Balls hit me in the head because I couldn't catch them, I was always picked last for the team and teased mercilessly. My instructors didn't think I'd last two weeks. Through sheer stubbornness and persistence, I trained over five years.

Four or five days a week, an hour and a half for every class, I channeled my intense feelings through punching and kicking. Transforming all the aggression into physical action saved me from completely losing my mind. I've never worked so hard or been so proud to pass a test. My pain tolerance increased through constant bruising, a black eye, and a broken toe. My balance, strength, and coordination improved by leaps and bounds. I ran and lifted weights, too. No longer feeling vulnerable, I sized up men as opponents.

Gradually my rage died down to a slow burn and I moved on emotionally after my divorce. Exercise became a routine part of my life until I had children which is another story for a different day. There are days when I feel intense frustration or anger and wish I could return to karate. I can't physically do it anymore but, once upon a time, I was a badass before it was a thing.

Prompted by Tracey Duncan.

REDISCOVERING WHAT WAS (SEPTEMBER 2019)

Before adulting was a word, before the internet and cell phones, I lived in Idaho after leaving Virginia with a one-way plane ticket sent with love and expectations. Then, I remained after our divorce with no house and no wheels. Living alone for the first time, with $500 in hand, I went car shopping.

My friend, Bruce and I looked at four cars but the 1963 Studebaker Lark was the only one that started. Sold! It was a classic car. I loved her personality. I didn't love the fact that parts were hard to find or that I couldn't afford to restore it. I called her Jimmi Lark.

Jimmi was old but I was young, able to run eight-minute miles, lift weights, practice martial arts. I lived on "Baltic Avenue" in a tiny, run-down duplex without a next-door neighbor. Tess, my big moon dog, and Byrd, my cat, kept me company.

In writing these words, I rediscovered feeling young, hopeful, and confused. It was a time of many firsts in my adult life. There was a lot of freedom in those five years between marriages, along with a lot of mistakes.

Prompted by Crystal Wood.

THE I FEEL FAT-UGLY-OLD GUIDE TO WELL BEING

Yes, I've been around the block a time or two, maybe three. I know what my self-talk patterns are really about.

Cycles of despair. Neural ruts. They sound like this:

I feel fat.

I hate myself.

If I eat, I'll feel better.

Not, really. If I eat too much then I can obsess over my eating habits and how fat I feel.

Maybe a diet will fix it.

But, before I go on a diet, I'll binge and get it all out of my system.

I feel sick.

I feel fat.

I hate myself.

I don't feel pretty.

She looks pretty.

How come I don't look as pretty as she does?

I wish I was pretty.

I wish I was young.

When I was pretty and young, I didn't think I was pretty.

When I was thinner, I felt fat.

Now I feel old.

You get the idea. Maybe this sounds vaguely familiar.

This kind of negative self-talk is a way of staying in denial. If you numb out with food, alcohol, drugs, gambling, sex, shopping, TV, etc., you are not acknowledging what's really happening.

Identifying the truth can be pretty terrifying. It might mean that something has to change.

It might mean doing something different.

Taking new action means not knowing what to expect and feeling weird because things are different. It won't feel comfortable.

But wait, it was already uncomfortable.

Well-being requires honesty. It takes guts to look below the surface at what's going on when the I-feel-fat-old-uglies act up.

It requires willingness to try something different and to stick with it even though it feels awkward.

Pay attention. Question your thoughts. Evaluate what you are saying. Would you talk to a friend or a loved one this way? If not, then the negative chatter needs to stop. Is what you're telling yourself even rational?

Practice self-compassion. Be nice to yourself. Be encouraging.

Soften the hard edges.

Use humor, if you can.

Ask for help. Talk to someone. Get therapy, if you need it. It's ok to ask.

Accept what is. Surrender to what you have no control over.

Get out of yourself and do something for someone else.

Stop comparing.

Feel the feelings, the real ones underneath the cycle. Write about them. Draw them. Dance them. Whatever it takes to feel, do it. The irony about feelings is that they begin to dissipate the minute you allow them to be. Avoiding them makes them bigger and more unmanageable.

Why is it so hard to recognize our own beauty?

Practice gratitude. Look for the "small mercies."

Look within, not without. Find something to believe in.

What is timeless and eternal? Focus on that.

We are the cosmos, the earth, the sky, deep blue and clear.

We're only here for a short, little while and we need to make the best of it.

ODE A TOOTHBRUSH

Not long ago I saw a great ad for toothbrushes in a women's fashion magazine:

Tall
Thin
Smart
Chic

Excuse me, what? One toothbrush can contain and manifest all of our most cherished beauty ideals?

According to current standards, I need at least $20,000+ to look sexy and get my dramatic transformation. I gave up trying to look younger and now I'm almost beyond repair. Apparently, I could benefit from Botox, fillers, surgery, injectables, and lasers. My skin! My jowls! My body!

Anti-aging propaganda is unnerving, appalling and reeks of racist, patriarchal attitudes toward women. Too much energy and money goes into this industry. If you haven't gotten serious about your wrinkles, pores, and skin texture, are you deeply flawed? Of course not! How has this become so important?

As a society, where are our priorities? What are our values?

Advertising for beauty doesn't usually contain one word about inner transformation, self-love, treating others compassionately or helping feed the poor. Forget about world peace. It's all about external appearance.

I'm certainly not opposed to looking and feeling good. I am opposed to the emphasis on these skewed priorities.

I've said it before. I'll say it again. We live on a tiny blue marble in the middle of vast cosmic space. The Earth is our home. We need to take care of our planet and each other. If we don't, we won't last as a species.

Will you say on your deathbed, "I wish I looked younger?"

I would much rather say that I'd lived and loved well.

BEAUTY BEYOND COMPARE (2017)

Body positive. Body negative. For women, body image is an extension of self-identity. More likely than not, our body images are distorted. It's important to relentlessly question our ideas and perceptions about our bodies. We need to challenge the messages we receive about our bodies. Remember that from the 12th century until the mid-19th century, a woman's legal and property rights belonged to her father or husband. This was common law relating to a wife's legal status. Despite years of effort to gain equality, women continue to be viewed as the property of men. To this day, women are fighting for full control of their own bodies without government interference.

It's no wonder, then, that in the microcosm of my life and, like every woman I know, I have a complicated relationship with my body. The first time I remember anyone commenting unfavorably about my body was when I was in Kindergarten. Girls giggled about my big legs. Five years old and my legs were not ok?

Throughout childhood, PE was always dreadful because my body was so uncoordinated. My mother told me, "You're just slow because you were born in the South." I believed it when I was a child but WTF kind of reasoning is that?

In third grade, I beat Phillip in a relay race. It was a highlight of my young life. Johnny put training wheels on his bike and let me ride it. That was cool, too. These are my two positive memories about being in my body as a young girl.

At age fifteen, when I was 5'5" and weighed 125, I thought I was too fat. I was still growing. My mother and I went on a diet together, my first one. I went out on a date with Robbie, my dreamboat, and he made fun of my legs being bigger than his. Of course, I felt bad about my legs, again. Now I wonder why I didn't just tell him he had some lame-ass skinny legs. Retorts like that weren't in my vocabulary then.

When I graduated from high school at eighteen, I was my adult height at 5'7" and weighed 133. I still thought I was fat, I guess because I had those huge damn legs. I dated someone who looked at a photo of me when I was five and said, "You always had those great legs." I didn't believe him. By then my negative body image was well-established.

Then came the "freshman fifteen." I "ballooned" to 150. My mother, ever obsessed about the size of my body, took me to a doctor who gave me HGC injections and put me on a five hundred calories a day diet. I stuck to it until I was down to 130. It's no surprise that I gained it all back. Thus started years of yoyo dieting accompanied by body dysmorphia. To this day, I can't tell if I'm bigger or smaller than someone else. I look at them and wonder, "Could I fit in their pants? Are they bigger than me? Smaller?"

Why do I even think this way? Precluding all the social and political issues, this obsession with appearance began with my parents. Both of them always talked about weight, theirs and mine, frequently commented on others and their appearance, and were constantly concerned with looking good.

Shortly before he died at 93, my dad told me, "I don't like Oprah anymore."

I asked, "Why not?" He replied, "She got fat."

This was before her latest iteration when she bought into Weight Watchers and disappointed many fans. How can one of the world's most successful and wealthy women on the planet still obsess about her weight? Women are judged more on appearance than we are by intelligence, skills, wealth, accomplishments or the way we treat others.

In my family, there was nothing worse than being fat. It mattered less if you were selfish or mean. Fat was the bottom of the barrel. Manners were very important, though. We had to have manners and behave at all times. Feelings were not ever expressed or talked about. Not ever.

After commenting about my own eating issues in an online discussion about the #Whole30 diet, I wondered, "When did I start eating emotionally?" I don't remember the very first time I ate because I felt anxious, depressed, nervous, or upset. I do know that when I got sober in 1995, I gained twenty pounds. It was cross-addictive behavior. I stopped numbing my feelings with alcohol which meant I could FEEL them. I couldn't escape them anymore. If I "used" food, I could obsess about my weight problem rather than experience my feelings.

Now I allow myself to feel what I'm feeling more often than not. I'm also aware at times of feeling upset and choosing to reach for food anyway, especially chocolate. It acts like a drug, it soothes me for a minute. I can't diet anymore. I know how to do it; however, after so many years of insanity around food and feelings, I can't stay psychologically healthy on a diet. I become overly obsessive about what I'm eating and how much. I start to feel crazy.

For the most part, despite of the occasional struggle with food to manage feelings, I accept my body the way it is today. Negative feelings that arise are not so much about my physical size as much as it is about my aging body – sagging skin, wrinkles, and age spots. The prevailing negative attitude about female aging is another insidious form of societal contempt towards women.

Even beautiful, famous women struggle with body issues. Marilyn Monroe, still considered one of the sexiest women ever, wrestled with her weight and self-image. When Jane Fonda was Barbarella, she was totally hot and bulimic. Her eating was disordered when she was making workout videos. In 2016, she stated in an interview that she started dieting in adolescence to please men, and in particular, her father. Misty Copeland, the first African American to become the principal ballerina for the American Ballet, admits to managing emotions with food. She said in an interview that she ate a dozen Krispy Kreme donuts in one sitting to manage her painful feelings of being the only woman of color in the troupe.

Conservative backlash against women has increased pressure on appearance in many ways. For example, the effort to control the shape of women's bodies is reflected in changing standards. The average height of a Playboy bunny, a stellar example of the perfect surgically enhanced female body, has increased while the average weight has decreased. This is true for Miss America as well. Photoshop manipulates female bodies and distorts what's normal. Models are slimmed down. Pores, wrinkles, and blemishes are eliminated.

So many women are dissatisfied with their bodies. Bring up dieting or body image and women will tell similar stories. When I consider the big picture, how women have been mistreated and abused, their basic human rights denied for centuries, I understand that my struggles are a tiny piece of an enormous puzzle. It's an act of rebellion to see ourselves as beautiful, inside and out. We resist by embracing and celebrating our own uniqueness.

All of us, in our infinite forms and colors, are beautiful beyond compare.

PORTALS OF AGING (2013)

Recently I was asked to write both about my experience of being in my fifties and my menopausal experiences. It's difficult for me to write in my authentic voice about this. My first reaction is to start doing research and then educate you, my dear reader. If I approach the question academically, then it removes me one step from my feelings. If I think about it, I don't feel it; however, most of these experiences are visceral, not cerebral.

Looking back two years at my first selfie, I can see how shy I was then, how inhibited I was about sharing myself, how uncomfortable I was in front of the camera. I'm different now.

I am standing on the boundary of a new territory. Turning 60 in April feels like a threshold event. I used to think that 60 was REALLY old but I don't feel as old as I thought I would. I feel like me - wiser, more purposeful, less angst-ridden. I know who I am.

There have been many changes on the spiral journey of my life.

First portal: Maiden

The feelings I've had throughout my journey as a woman are as complex and varied as the stars. I didn't get my period until I was nearly 15. I was so worried that something was wrong with me. I wanted to be like the other girls. I wanted to know what they were talking about.

As a Maiden, I had romantic and foolish notions about becoming a W-O-M-A-N! Once I started my period, I was repulsed by the mess and the (omg) thick, uncomfortable pads and (OMG!) belts and buckles. I was worried about the smell and the "accidents" and bleeding all over my sheets at night.

When I turned 30, I started getting terrible pre-menstrual symptoms. I went to see my doctor because I didn't know why I was having extreme mood swings with such terrible irritability. HE informed me that PMS "is a disease we have been treating for 10 years." I never went back to see him. I was offended that he referred to being born female as a disease.

I was at my physical peak in my early 30s. I trained in martial arts for five years, could run an 8-minute mile, and lifted weights in the gym with the college football players. I feel sad to remember that I still believed I was fat when I was at my most lean and fit, but body dysmorphia is a topic for another day.

Second portal: Mother

I am in awe of the sacred blood of women, the life-affirming blood we possess. We bleed without dying. We can create new life and become a Mother. I'm happy that mothers are beginning to teach their daughters to celebrate their menses and are creating special rituals for them.

In deference to all the women who struggle with fertility issues, I hope this passage is not too painful to read. I almost want to apologize for the ease with which I was able to get pregnant. For years I tried not to get pregnant but when I felt ready to have children, it didn't take long. I was 35 when I had my first daughter and 38 when I had my second. At that time I didn't know I was tempting the gods by waiting for so long. I was fortunate that conception wasn't a problem and for that, I am truly grateful.

I enjoyed my 40s. I was a mother of young children who worked, exercised, and maintained a garden. I had so much energy. When my children were 4 and 6, because of my husband's income, I was able to quit working and stay home. Motherhood was all-consuming. I took them to dance classes and piano lessons, and became their Girl Scout leader. We did a lot of fun things together as a family, too.

Third portal: Crone? Not yet!

My daughters began going through puberty about the same time I began having menopausal symptoms. My first hot flash occurred on my oldest daughter's 15th birthday. The girls experienced puberty going forward, confused by their changing bodies. I felt like I was going through puberty backwards and was equally confused by my changing body.

These physical changes are life-altering. The body is in charge. No amount of wishing makes it any other way. The mood swings worsened as I lurched through my cycles and became irregular. Night sweats caused insomnia. I woke up at 2 a.m. nightly for months. And then, the weird stuff I never heard about began – sensitivity to smells, motion sickness when never before, and lactose intolerance. Simultaneously, weird stuff I had heard of before appeared – the loss of libido, dry and wrinkling skin, chin hairs, and age spots.

After a year of not sleeping, I tried Hormone Replacement Therapy (HRT). It turned out to be heavenly. Suddenly I had a life without hormonal mood swings. My depression dissipated. I stopped taking the pills after five years because of the health risks, but it sure was a sweet ride while it lasted.

There was a pivotal moment one night in my early 50s. My husband and my oldest daughter were working and my youngest was away on a cross-country team trip. I was home alone in the evening for the first time in eons. I realized that soon both girls would be driving, branching out, and moving away as children will do. For over thirteen years, I stayed at home with them. My life revolved around them. I thought, "If I don't do something before they are gone from the house, I will go nuts with an empty nest."

I kept my eye on the want ads and one day I applied for a part-time job. Next thing I knew, I was working again. With dismay, I realized that both girls were still at home and I had twice as much to do. They still needed me. I had forgotten what it was like to try and juggle everything.

On the job, being older was a perk. I had experience that I could share with my younger co-workers. I didn't "sweat" my peculiar boss because I was old enough to be his mother. He just didn't intimidate me. I had skills and education that helped me build an awesome community program from scratch.

A lot of friends told me it was "all downhill after 50," but my physical downhill hit at 55 in Kathmandu,

Nepal. I was in a hotel bathroom, looking down at my thighs and appalled that they had turned into cottage cheese. I thought, rather innocently, "I must be retaining water from the airplane trip." No. We went from Nepal to Bhutan where there is no flat land anywhere, except for the airport runway in Paro. My knees were killing me by the end of the trip. My knees and legs will never be the same.

I worked for four years before I stopped wanting to work for someone else. I discovered that when the ovaries quit producing estrogen so does the overwhelming urge to take care of other people, animals and plants. I had no clue until I read *The Wisdom of Menopause* by Christiane Northrup. She explained that when the hormones disappear, so does the desire to meet everyone else's needs. I found this rather shocking and I believe it was an unpleasant shift for my family as well.

A new third portal: Queen

Thanks to Donna Henes, author of *The Queen of My Self: Stepping Into Sovereignty in Midlife*, I know now that I've entered into a stage between Mother and Crone. Because of improved nutrition and medical care, women are living longer. If we're fortunate to remain healthy, we have gained an extra twenty years of life, years our grandmothers and mothers might not have experienced. Women in this stage of life are part of the most educated and influential group of women ever.

This is a significant time of transition for many women. I, too, am becoming the Queen of Myself. I'm not yet a grandmother nor am I elderly. It's a time of PMZ, post-menopausal zest.

Note: In 2014 I decided I wanted to help "Zesty Women in their Third Age" feel great about what's next in life and greet it with enthusiasm. The header on my website was "A Guiding Light for Sublimely Brazen Aging Women." With a unique combination of photography, journaling, and spirituality plus a dash of counseling skills, I started a coaching business online.

Unfortunately, now 70, I learned, like everything else, that this zesty phase doesn't last. And neither did my business.

LIFE FLOWS ON IN A QUANTUM STATE OF MIND

Since writing about the portals of aging, I've been in a quantum physics state of mind.

I am fascinated by light. Light is a particle. Light is a wave. This incredible aspect of light is referred to as wave-particle duality. The behavior of light depends on the observer. The observer changes reality.

We filter our own reality through our senses and mental perceptions. We can change our reality through observation.

Even more astonishing is the notion of quantum non-locality, the idea that the same particle can exist in two locations at once. If this is true, it allows for faster-than-light communication!

Each of us is a drop of water in the vast ocean.

We are the drop.
We are the ocean.

Evaluating Memories and Moving Forward

Memories are portals, gates, or doors that lead toward understanding. Every stage of development teaches us something if we pay attention to the lessons; but, our memories are affected by who we are and whom we have become.

A maiden is (hopefully) innocent about the world. What do you recall about being a child? What stories do you cherish from your maidenhood? Were you innocent or robbed of your innocence? What aspects of your childhood do you carry with you?

Mother does not necessarily imply that you bear children. We are capable of creating all kinds of projects. What projects have you created as an adult that you love? Is there anyone you have "mothered?"

The Queen stands in own power when she cares less about what other people think. Her wings unfurl. She feels increasing communion with Spirit. If you have reached this stage of life, do you feel your strength emerging? If you haven't reached this stage, how do you see yourself growing into it? What do you imagine for yourself as you age?

I have great role models for aging. My grandmother told me she loved being 80. She could say or do whatever she wanted and nobody said a word about it because she was 80.

My mother, Joanne Turney Bauers, created and published her own book, *The Art of Joyful Aging*. It is filled with her paintings and quotes from friends and family about getting older. She started painting when she was in her 50s after my sister and I left home. She said that she felt like she had so much less time to waste than the younger students and was, therefore, much more motivated to paint.

I feel the constraint of time too. How will I spend the time that remains? It's a question many baby boomers are asking themselves.

Acceptance leads to Presence

At any stage of growth, acceptance is the key. Learning to accept the present as it is, ourselves as we are and the people around us as they are gives us great freedom. It increases our emotional health and spiritual progress. If we are not fighting with ourselves internally, criticizing others, or wishing for something else, we can remain in the present.

Presence in the moment creates a feeling of expansiveness. That expansive feeling can also generate fear. Do you know that love and fear cannot occupy the same space? Do you love yourself as you are? Do you treat yourself with compassion? I know how difficult it is to do.

Perhaps using quantum mechanics to explain the portals of aging is ridiculous. Maybe not, but what I do know is that what used to seem impossible isn't anymore. When I was a kid, I loved watching the Jetsons. They could see each other on the telephone. It didn't seem possible then but now we have Skype, FaceTime, and Zoom.

We are all in this together. I need guides to help me with my wounds and scars and I am a guide, too. I can remember being young and confused and simultaneously I am older. Am I a wave or a particle?

Sometimes I go with the flow. Sometimes I get stuck. When I write, I feel the ink flow onto the paper. When I type, I feel the keyboard under my fingertips. When you read my post, my thoughts appear in your mind. It's all incredible and miraculous.

I seek to understand the truth and the nature of reality.

What do you seek?

ON BEING 61 (2014)

I am 61 years old. Sometimes I squirm in my chair, feeling awkward in my changing body. I wonder if I've made valid decisions about life, work, and children. I've made mistakes. I have a few regrets. I wonder how things might have been different.

Driving down the road, looking in the rearview mirror, I see that the road behind me stretches farther back than the one ahead.

The passing of time appears linear but it's quite elastic. As a teenager, the thought of living to age 61 was unimaginable

As a parent, there were nights that felt eternal when one of my babies was sick and crying for hours. There were days that seemed like they would never end when chasing two girls as toddlers, constantly trying to keep them from harm. Tension created by adolescent drama made an hour feel like months. Suddenly, they were off to college, graduating and starting their own lives. Now, I look back at the past and the time seems fleeting. I've lived in different places, in changing political eras, and raised children all in the blink of an eye.

Chronologically, time doesn't go faster as I age but it does feel that way. It's the same 60 seconds, 60 minutes, 24 hours I've always had. If I stay present and mindful, time does slow down momentarily. I've spent many years working on understanding myself, our family dynamics, learning to communicate, how to be emotionally, psychologically, and spiritually healthy.

In the future, I expect to be better at practicing lovingkindness, compassion, and mindfulness. I understand the constancy of change. I've learned skills to help me cope with change. I have a relationship with nature that guides me through lunar cycles and solar seasons. Curiosity and creativity provide me with the incentive to continue to grow. I know that I'm part of everything, I'm made of stardust. My inner strength increases as I weather challenges and some of the ravages of time.

Should I be blessed to live until a ripe old age, I believe that my inner world will expand as my outer existence contracts. The road will become more narrow until eventually it's a footpath I take as I let go and experience death as another form of birth.

HAVE I OVARY-REACTED? (2014)

Turns out I have a love-hate relationship with my ovaries. I love that I was able to get pregnant and bring two amazing, smart, and beautiful daughters into the world. There have been times, though, that I haven't felt the hormonal love.

Back in the '60s, no one talked about Sacred Blood Mysteries. Fifth grade health education did not prepare me for life with my ovaries. No one ever mentioned their "vajayjays." Eve Ensler hadn't written The Vagina Monologues. The Red Tent movement hadn't begun. The birth control pill was available but was still considered controversial.

From ages 14 to 51, my ovaries took me on a roller coaster ride ruled by hormonal mood shifts and drama. I didn't start menstruating until I was almost 15. I was embarrassed about my delayed development. Once I got my period, the pristine fantasy of becoming a woman was over. Cramps, massive amounts of bleeding, and those disgusting belts and pads were agonizing. I just knew everyone else knew what was happening. It was so uncomfortable sitting on that brick of padding. Thank heavens my best friend told me about tampons. It took a while to figure out how to use them. Women who menstruate know the embarrassment of unexpected bleeding on clothes and bedsheets. It's triple mortifying as a teen.

Eventually, I adjusted. It wasn't too complicated until I started having major mood swings as I approached 30. I went to a male doctor who informed me that I had a disease they'd been treating for ten years called

Pre-Menstrual Syndrome. I wondered what women did during the eons before doctors figured it out. Insulted for being diagnosed with the disease of being born female, I never went back.

I became pregnant and delivered our first daughter at age 35 and our second daughter at age 38. There are good reasons to have children younger when you have more energy. As an older mother, I was diagnosed with "advanced maternal age." I was lucky I didn't have fertility problems, but going without a solid night's sleep for five years just about did me in. I went in to see someone about my depression when I could not. stop. crying. The female Physician's Assistant regarded me kindly and prescribed something. I stayed on antidepressants for the next five years.

When I entered peri-menopause, my mood shifts became extreme. The first two weeks of my cycle weren't bad but then as soon as I ovulated, the rest of the cycle was miserable. I felt like black blood was running through my veins. Everyone and everything challenged my patience. I lurched through my cycle every month. I felt batshit crazy for days on end. My cycles became increasingly erratic.

On the day of my oldest daughter's 15th birthday, I got my first hot flash. It started at my knees and slowly traveled up my body until my head felt like it was on fire. With three hormonal females in the family, my poor husband was drowning in an estrogen tsunami.

The medical community has neglected to study women's bodies for decades because female hormones complicate the studies. They study men because their hormones don't fluctuate. This bias leads doctors to study and test drugs only in men. Only recently has research considered both genders. Because of this women are at risk for incorrect diagnoses, misinformed treatments, sickness, and even death. Current mainstream reproductive treatments put us at risk for breast cancer, heart disease, stroke, and blood clots.

We are woefully uninformed about the Wise Woman tradition, our own blood mysteries. These mysteries teach us to remember that women bleed and do not die. Our blood is the blood of nourishment. The how and why these traditions are lost is a long, heart-breaking story for another day.

There is a terrible discrepancy between Western medicine and women's mysteries. The battle for reproductive freedom wages on. My story only scratches the surface. It's my hope that by telling our stories and sharing our wisdom that we can restore honor to our mysteries.

ONE DECADE AT A TIME

On April 3, 2015, I turned 62. I'm a little bit compulsive about self-evaluation. I'm very curious about developmental stages. We all have similarities and differences but there are general trends in human behavior, especially if we look for our similarities.

I wonder, how it is possible to look back so far, yet experience my life as a short amount of time? This rubber band of time seems to expand and contract. In absolute reality, time only exists in relation to other objects and people but that is most certainly another topic.

I decided to take a little trip down memory lane decade by decade. Memory is a funny thing. Mine is a little unreliable and occasionally best aided by Google.

Age 2. We lived in Valley Forge, PA. I became a big sister. My mother had a nurse come in and help. When the nurse was leaving, I said, "Don't forget the baby." Apparently, I didn't understand my sister was there to stay.

I didn't have any perspective on my life at this age. I suppose I lived in the moment which is easier to do as a toddler than it is now. I was a cute little kid with curly hair.

Age 12. We lived in northern Virginia. My grandmother, bless her generous heart, took my sister and two cousins, Margie and Cathy, to the World's Fair in NYC. We had such a good time! We stayed in the Waldorf Astoria. The Fair's theme was "Peace

Through Understanding" and the price of admission for adults was $2. It's a Small World was my favorite exhibit.

My body was beginning to change but I hadn't started menstruating yet. I had physical and emotional growing pains. No one explained what was happening to me. I remember feeling very awkward and uncomfortable.

Age 22. I was in Charlottesville, attending the University of Virginia but hadn't yet declared my major. I took 3 semesters off to find myself and then returned, but I really had no clue what I wanted to do when I grew up. It was a cataclysmic year. My first love died suddenly. Even though our relationship was extremely troubled, I was devastated and lost in so many ways.

I was young and pretty, with long blond hair and a wild spirit. Because of Casey's sudden death, I decided that there was no point in making plans because it was possible to die suddenly. I lived on a precarious edge for years. I became a free spirit, pretty much going where the wind blew me.

Age 32. I moved to Idaho, got married and divorced. I was tired of working in sandwich shops, so I returned to school to get a Masters in Counseling. I discovered a lot about myself and my relationships. I lived alone for the first time.

I learned in school that not making a decision was a decision in itself. What a pivotal moment. Adulthood seemed attainable as I began to slowly mature. I was in the best physical shape of my life but didn't know it then.

Age 42. I was remarried and living in Utah with two small children, and working as a rural mental health therapist when I made another big decision. I stopped working to stay at home with our daughters. I was surprised at the reaction from some of my friends when I said that I quit work. They gave me the "stink eye," as if I had done something wrong.

It was a difficult adjustment in terms of feeling valued as a contributing member of society. Somehow, mothering seemed like a "less than" choice. The myth of Superwoman was still alive and well. As women, we need to support each other, whether or not we have children, whether we work outside the home or not.

I didn't have a mid-life crisis, but I did experience a spiritual bottom. Outwardly my life seemed wonderful, but inside I was in a lot of pain. Eventually, I chose the path of sober living and chose to learn how to live life on life's terms one day at a time. Opening up spiritually changed my life.

Age 52. I was a mother to two teen girls and going through menopause. Holy hormonal hell. It was pretty bumpy. There was no Red Tent movement where we could gloriously celebrate our changing bodies. Nothing prepared me for teenagers but we all survived.

Everyone says becoming a parent changes your life. It changed me on a cellular level. I am not the person I would have been without my children. I'm very grateful that I was able to raise them and then release them into the world as wonderful, caring, and smart young adults.

Age 62. My husband retired and we moved to his hometown in Wyoming. Finally, I feel like I know who I am and what I want to do when I grow up. All the years of self-examination, spiritual growth, family relationships, and evolving friendships have helped me become who I am today. I'm just getting started on my Third Age, looking for ways to continue growing and helping other women to do the same.

I accept myself for who I am. Yes, there are wrinkles and a few physical limitations. It's part of the privilege of getting older. I want to dive deeper into more important things. I plan on staying engaged with life and people.

Yes, I guess this has been all about me, but I do know that I'm not the center of the universe. I'm just one person doing the best I can on a daily basis. I'm excited to see what happens next.

With any luck, I could be around to write about the next three or four decades. Who knows what I'll have to say about that! Any guesses?

SUBLIMELY BRAZEN AGING (2019)

Five years ago I wrote about being sixty-one.

Five years is a short time.
Five years is a long time.
Five years is an arbitrary amount of time, like my age.

Sixty-six.

I've been alive for over 24,000 days, living them one day at a time. One moment at a time.

Five years ago I didn't know what the future held, unaware of the tsunami of change about to hit my life. Within eight months, I lost my beloved Irish wolfhound, half my thyroid, and my dad, in that order. Then we moved to another state. My community, my support system, and my dream home were left behind. Our oldest daughter moved to Portland, Oregon, and our youngest to Thailand for six months. I was a mess, wracked by grief I thought I was handling just fine, thank you very much. I felt like a plant yanked out by the roots, left dangling in dirty clumps, limp, drying out in the sun.

There were signs I wasn't fine. A major depressive episode in 2016 was one of them. I pulled out of it eventually but when another one threatened to drop me into the abyss, I went back into counseling.

I'm a retired therapist but I didn't want to need help. I went in anyway and cried for months, pouring out feelings about the past, my childhood, politics, trauma, feeling like a failure. A sympathetic, unbiased listener is worth EVERYTHING. All that was stuck started to loosen.

Every week I received an assignment. Every week I paid attention and wrote in my journal. I signed up for Pilates classes. As soon as the weather allowed, I went hiking with my dog Hoover, seeking and finding solace in nature. I took two watercolor painting classes at the local art center.

My creative juices began to flow again. I can see now that efforts to create an online coaching business and write two books were not failures. They were learning experiences. I took creative risks. I'm someone who is willing to learn all the time. I'm kinder to myself about my efforts now.

Three weeks ago we started remodeling a large section of our house. We took it all down to the studs and discovered internal structural problems. Every little thing torn apart will be reconstructed, all new, stronger, and better than before. It will be the same space but different.

Counseling was my remodeling process. I dismantled my past. I'm coming back together. Like the house, the finishing touches aren't done yet. I reframed a lot of my negative self-talk, reinforced my boundaries, and began again.

As long as I live, I'll reach for the proverbial Brass Ring. I seek success in my own best form of vitality – exuberant, fully alive and coherent, buzzing with my electric inner power. Undefined by anyone else. Creating what pleases me. Speaking my truth.

OLD AGE IS NOT A DISEASE (2014)

It's all relative.

According to the *Encyclopedia Britannica*, the average life span in ancient Rome and medieval Europe was between 20 and 30 years. Our life expectancy in 1900 was around 65. It has increased 25 years in the last century. So, God willin' and the creek don't rise, we can make it to 90 and beyond.

The medical community treats these bonus years as an illness. The prognosis is grim and full of admonitions about weight gain, insomnia, senility or dementia, osteoporosis, and heart disease, not to mention the need for hearing aids, dentures or joint replacements. It's all about the pathology of aging.

Advertisers struggle to meet the often unarticulated needs of older consumers who have been largely ignored by brand managers, marketers, and product designers. The problem with most "solve" products is that they highlight and reinforce the debilitating effects of aging. The pathology of aging appears to be a common thread.

Gerontophobia is the fear of growing old, or a hatred or fear of the elderly. We fear what we don't understand.

Admittedly, I feared aging when I was much younger. I didn't know what to expect. It's no wonder, given the emphasis on youth in our culture, that I anticipated the worst. My aging happened a little bit at a time until one day I looked down at my body, in the mirror and wondered what happened.

Finally, we are starting to notice that there are benefits to aging. Who knew?

Older people are more relaxed and generally happier. We get better at the business of living through experience in the school of hard knocks. We become wiser, more insightful, and more appreciative of the good things in life. Studies show that long-term memory stays intact. The brain is far more elastic than previously believed so it's possible to learn new skills.

As we age, we will continue to behave as we have always behaved as adults. If we take the time to assess our behaviors, we can change that which is no longer useful or functional. Age is merely chronology, the arrangement of events or dates in the order of their occurrence. We are never static.

Women, in particular, thrive in community with each other. We are discovering that we want not only to consciously age but to share our experiences, hopes, and dreams with each other. The aging process can be both positive and challenging but we will be able to improve our coping skills with mutual support. Connecting with each other is key to our mental and physical health.

We're not denying aging. We want to understand the process. We want to stay present through all the changes. We can accept the changes we experience.

We learn self-compassion through dialogue with others. It's easier to acknowledge someone else's suffering before our own. If we respond with kindness and understanding to another, then perhaps we can treat ourselves more kindly, too.

Telling our stories is a joyful experience, we have so much to share. There is great mystery in this sacred transition. We can learn to embrace it and celebrate the gifts we bring to light with each other.

TO KNOW SORROW (2014)

I had premonitions. Fears. Dreams. But it was still a shock, hearing those words, "Yes, he's dead." Irrevocable words.

Casey was 21 years old. Forty years later, he is still 21 years old. Never older, not wiser. Gone forever. He didn't return from that trip to the west coast.

The sight of his body in a casket is a more vivid memory at times than the ones of him alive when he was laughing, strong, vibrant.

We weren't really broken up but we were apart. It was complicated. In 1975 there were no cell phones. He didn't call me on the telephone but he did write once. I had a terrible feeling when I read his letter that I'd never see him again. I didn't.

The relationship was abusive. It was before the words domestic violence became commonplace. The abuse was alcohol-related. He was different when he was sober. Smart. Funny. He was mean when he was drunk.

We met in high school. His best friend was shot and killed in a random act of violence, something that was much less common then than it is now. The killer was never found. Casey's golden eyes were filled with pain and sorrow. I was a goner for the wounded boy in a man's body.

Four years later, he was gone, too. I remember the gut-wrenching agony, the broken-hearted sobs, the chaos that ensued for years as I sought comfort in drugs, alcohol, and doomed relationships. I had the physical sensation of a cannonball-sized hole in my chest for a long time. Nothing could fill it.

When I remember his death, I feel sad but it's not painful anymore. Most of the time, it's a distant memory of a first love. And an awareness of the many things I learned about life and myself.

Because I was very young when this rug was pulled out from under me, I decided to stop making plans. What was the point? I was going to die anyway. It was years before I realized that maybe I wasn't going to die soon after all.

My search for spiritual answers to questions about life began. It's an ongoing quest to this day. No one talked about grief. No one I knew, anyway. I didn't know how to ask for help. Nobody offered either.

There were all "the firsts" – holidays, birthdays, anniversaries – that occurred without him. There were thoughts and feelings I wanted to share but I couldn't. Then over time, as the intensity lessened, I realized how much he wasn't going to experience, what he didn't know, couldn't know, would never know about life on Earth.

Summer's Sorrow

When I lived in Idaho, I trained in Korean martial arts. It was a revolutionary act of perseverance for me. I became close to my instructors as friends (and even married one of them!)

In 2014 an unlikely chain of events occurred with two of my former teachers. Vern, in Pennsylvania, and Kelly, in Idaho, passed away within days of each other. Even though we were no longer close, it was a reminder of our history together and the fragility of life. Their memorials occurred on the same day.

Partly because of the reminder about how short life can be, my husband and I decided to go on what I called a #3G adventure – great, grand, and glorious. We cruised the Baltic Sea before heading to Africa on Safari. Dreams do come true. I was looking forward to telling my friend Esther that I was going to be in her "neighborhood."

Esther Garvi, lived in Niger, Africa. She helped farmers grow indigenous plants for food. She also started a school for orphans, fulfilling her mother's dream. She was on her way home from Sweden in August when the car she was riding in rolled over and killed her. I thought I'd contact her after she arrived in Zinder, but she never made it.

In September, as we were returning home from Zimbabwe and Botswana, a young and successful entrepreneur, Scott Dinsmore, was killed while climbing Mt. Kilamanjaro. His sudden death triggered so many old feelings of grief. It took me some time to realize that in a strange way, I was reliving my past.

Recently I heard the Toto song, Africa, on the radio and thought of Scott posting Instagram photos. He and his beautiful wife were traveling for a year around the world after having sold everything. He was setting an example, walking his talk. His family, friends and online community are still reeling. His wife, Chelsea, and the Live Your Legend Team are providing an incredible amount of support to each other. It's wonderful to see them reach out in spite of their own personal pain.

My sense of loss has not been as intense as what I experienced forty years ago. I've had to learn healthier coping skills. I know that recovery from loss is a long process. I can still get knocked over by waves of emotion when a death occurs.

The Process of Grieving

Grief is a multifaceted response to loss, particularly to the loss of someone or something that has died, to which a bond or affection was formed. Although conventionally focused on the emotional response to loss, it also has physical, cognitive, behavioral, social, and philosophical dimensions. ~ Wikipedia

Grief is not the same experience for everyone. The 5 stages of grief described by Elizabeth Kübler-Ross were actually based on interviews with terminally ill people, not people who were grieving the loss of a loved one. Validating studies were never done. either. Fortunately, theories about grieving are improving along with our understanding of the process.

It is now recognized that grief is more than sorrow and emotional turmoil. Five common reactions are receiving particular attention in the mental health community.

Stress reactions include changes in physiological function that can increase one's vulnerability to illness and exacerbate preexisting physical problems.

Perception and thought are also affected, with the increased possibility of making impulsive and potentially harmful decisions and becoming more at risk for accidents.

A spiritual crisis often occurs, in which the guiding assumptions and values are called into question.

Family and communal response to loss, often neglected in the past, is a significant factor in grief and grief recovery.

Although the pain of loss may be universal, cultural heritage and influences and current support systems have much influence on the way one expresses and copes with stress.

The longer we live, the more likely it is that we will lose family and friends. Death is an unavoidable part of life. What happens is that over time we develop a grief history. How we deal with each loss is based on cumulative experience. Every loss triggers thoughts and feelings related to the past. If we learn how to cope with grief in a healthy manner, it becomes a valuable life skill. Grieving is a long, life-altering process. It's important to not only respect the process but to allow feelings to surface, not to push them aside or try to numb them. Reach out for help. It's available.

Friends and family will continue to die. We're born. We die. If we're lucky, a lot happens in between. I don't believe we should be so surprised by death. It's going to happen. Yes, it's a shock when it's unexpected, but it's also inevitable. It's an experience that changes us.

If you are grieving, view your journey with compassion for the person you were before and the person you are now. Grief transforms us in unexpected ways. Don't linger too long in the past, allow yourself to learn from it.

MUSINGS AND MYSTERIES

Odyssey into the Night

SHIFTING THE PARADIGM

Frankly, I'm tired of systemic colonial thoughts and ideas. Exhausted by it, really.

We need to shift the paradigm.

Elisabet Sahtouris, Ph.D., is an evolutionary biologist and futurist. She wrote a brilliant essay, Towards a Future Global Science: Axioms for Modeling a Living Universe. Her essay changed my perspective on scientific (male), mechanistic models of the cosmos. She offers a more optimistic, life-affirming design. I embrace her feminine perspective - one of co-creation with the universe.

As a woman, I am by nature, cyclical. My state of being is indivisible from nature. There is consciousness in nature. The natural world is my guide for wisdom, intuition, and creativity.

Sistering, perceiving women as allies, offers me cheer, comfort, and encouragement. Studies show that women tend and befriend each other when under stress. (Taylor, 2014.) We give encouragement, offer comfort, and provide hope, and reassurance. We also need to work through generations of distrust and fear.

Women's circles are growing. We are gathering and speaking out against predation and violence. We are creating intentional spaces to talk about white fragility and racism, striving to become more inclusive, however uncomfortable or awkward it might be.

I believe the antidote to despair is in possibility. Creativity, the act of creation, is life-affirming. I will not resign myself to despair. Instead, I encourage women to weave a vibrant tapestry out of our brilliance.

In the early 1980's, I became part of the second wave of feminism. My thinking was influenced by Mary Daly, Starhawk, Z Budapest, Anne Kent Rush, Barbara Walker, and more. Their insight and remarkable writings about Judeo-Christian tradition and patriarchy in religion caused me to leave the religion of my childhood, Christianity as experienced through the Episcopal Church.

Historical trauma left over from The Burning Times made me nervous to openly speak about my shifting beliefs. I was a solitary practitioner of my own brand of neo-paganism. For years I only read books by women in order to compensate for a lifetime of reading books by men about their points of view.

What I learned then differs from what is being written about by intelligent, thoughtful women now. I try to keep up with the academic jargon and intellectual discourse about social and political issues emerging in rapid fire on social media. Our culture is changing at lightning speed.

When I read the headline, "Divine Feminine is sexist," by willow on Medium.com, I felt exhausted, and then I was mad. I'm calm now and have thought about this a lot. I don't agree that the term, Divine Feminine, in and of itself reinforces gender stereotypes of femininity.

When I entered recovery in a 12-step program, I struggled with archaic language, patriarchal concepts, and vestiges of Christianity to find a way toward a "God of my own understanding." In my mind at that time, the word God was sexist. Eventually, I came to believe in "a power greater than myself" and now follow a spiritual path that's very fluid.

Spiritual systems of belief (religions) have theories, histories, and institutions that are built around the tenets of their system. Divine Feminine can merely be a description of life force or creativity. As a matter of balance, there needs to be the energy of action, or what can be referred to as Divine Masculine. Humans will heap meaning upon meaning in all of this and then create rules to go along with behaviors and punishments or consequences for not following the rules.

According to Buddhist philosophy, none of this inherently exists in absolute reality, but that is an entirely different discussion.

The bottom line for me, and this might get me into trouble, is that so much criticism is divisive. I agree calling out sexism and patriarchal systems needs to be done. Education and awareness will shift the paradigm eventually; however, personally, I can't afford to be in a constant state of rage like I was thirty-five years ago. I prefer to agree to disagree and then work towards the collective good in ways that make sense to me.

I do wonder, though, will we ever "Live and Let Live" in peace and harmony?

Note: Five years later my bottom line sounds privileged and insensitive to racism. It's not meant to be. My viewpoint has changed radically.

MOONDAY MUSINGS #10

A few days ago, I was caught by surprise when I teleported into the past. Driving down the street, minding my own business, Aqualung by Jethro Tull came on the radio. Suddenly I was 19 for a while.

These sudden jumps into an alternate reality never fail to amaze me. My 64-year-old self is surprised when non-linear experiences happen. I'm not surprised that they do happen but they can be momentarily disorienting.

Time is just the strangest thing. It really is all in my mind - these memories of 1972 are my own.

I lived on Jefferson Avenue in Charlottesville, Virginia. I was attending the University of Virginia without a clue about why I was there. I think I was supposed to find a husband. My mother encouraged me to study in the law library, or the medical library, so I could find a good husband with a bright financial future.

I met my first husband when I was hitchhiking home from school in 1976. That's another story. It's easy to jump time frames.

Brinkley and Betty were my roommates. We lived in a small, two bedroom apartment. Brinkley paid extra to have her own room with a double bed. I don't remember ever cleaning the apartment. Maybe we did. Our neighbor decorated his apartment with psychedelic posters that glowed in the black lights he used. We partied a lot in those days. We said things like far out and copacetic.

When I dropped out the second semester of my second year, I got a job in the French department as a secretary. It helped that I studied French for years in school. I never learned to speak it, though.

A professor came running in one day exclaiming, "I need someone in the 14th century!" I don't know if he ever found anyone there. He was lost in another time frame.

What I love remembering is the feeling of being young and feeling good. I miss that feeling sometimes. I thought I knew everything then. Now I know that I don't know much at all and that's okay.

MOONDAY MUSINGS #15

Progress.

What is it?

How do you define it for yourself?

The dictionary defines it as moving onward through space and time, making headway.

I've been doing that as a writer.

Looking back, I've been writing through many online iterations.

My first online presence was as mountain mama at Many Rivers to Cross. I was an enthusiastic participant in Sky Watch Friday. It was fun meeting nature photographers from all over the world. They inspired me to practice photography.

In 2011 I quit my day job, abandoned Many Rivers, and launched Loran's Heart. I produced three Journeys:

A Spiral Journey book with tips on journaling

A Transformation Journey for creating personal change

A Seeker's Journey e-course for spiritual growth

I didn't succeed financially but I learned a lot.

After that, I launched LoranHills.com. I wanted to be a life coach. I have a Masters degree in Counseling and a lot of life experience. The competition was fierce. I didn't know enough about marketing.

I focused on women and aging and generated some good interest in my group Skin Deepest. I didn't know how to maintain the momentum and ended up "sideways in the ditch" (as Fabeku Fatunmise describes it). It was a creative rough patch.

Unwilling to give up, I thought perhaps writing a wisdom book or memoir would be the best method for sharing my experience, strength, and hope. I kept writing but I couldn't settle on a theme or direction that worked.

During this time, I was volunteering for Treesisters and learning about feminine, nature-based leadership. I started to wonder what the world would look like if we could bring the feminine principle of life into balance with our unbalanced masculine world. Along came NaNoWriMo and in November I drafted a fictional novel incorporating many of my ideas about nature and life.

All along I've been writing, honing my skills as a writer. I'm teaching myself to write fiction. I'm learning about plot development, character traits, arc, tone, settings, pace, scenes. There's a lot to learn.
This is progress as I see it. I'm motivated by my desire to learn and create.

I've been hanging out in Instagram with a group of energetic and enthusiastic Young Adult writers in their twenties. I turn 65 in April. I wasn't capable of writing a book when I was that age but I am now. That's progress, not perfection.

A WOMAN'S PLACE

Long ago I had a photograph on my wall of an older woman gazing out her window. The caption said, "I can't believe I forgot to have children." At age thirty, I almost had my tubes tied because I didn't think I'd ever want children. By thirty-five, I delivered my first daughter and at thirty-eight I birthed my second. I worked as a rural mental health therapist until they were six and four.

The decision to quit work was difficult. I spent years getting my education and building a career. It was hard to let go of it all. What surprised me most, though, was the response from a few of my friends who seemed appalled by my decision. Women have the right to decide how they want to raise their children. Fortunately, I had the financial freedom to make that choice.

Staying home to raise my daughters is something I will never regret. I was able to do things with them and for them, I wouldn't have been able to do if I'd been working. At the same time, it didn't generate income. The first thing I did after I quit my job was clean out the closets. I felt compelled to validate my worth. I was at loose ends until I gained new unpaid employment while we built our dream house. Supervising construction became my job for eight months.

Our society values money, lots of it, as a primary symbol of success. Unfortunately, if a woman's place is in the home, and she has no financial power, then it puts her in a vulnerable position. Raising children properly is not viewed as a "real" job. Having seen the tragic results of child abuse and neglect, I would argue otherwise.

Over time, my perception of my place in the world shifted. We built that dream home in the country. Situated on 20 acres, bordered by BLM and Forest Service lands, there was room to roam. It was a slice of heaven for me, one I often dreamed of having.

I didn't get to spend time in nature growing up. I grew up in a city. I got in trouble once for playing in the woods on the way home from school because there were "escaped convicts" in there. Maybe a prisoner from a road crew disappeared once but I was sentenced to stay close to home. Our children's home was a special place for them to be safe playing outside, building forts, and sledding in the snow.

It was there, in Castle Cove, that I fell in love with the land. I learned to listen, observe and feel nature. Sagebrush, cedar, and juniper trees, wildflowers, deer, fox, skunks, raccoons, mountain lions, bears, moose all inhabited this alpine desert. I observed the paths of the sun and moon as they changed from solstice to equinox and back. Best of all, I walked the land in all directions, in all seasons, at all times of day and night. For the first time in my life, I grew deep roots. Never had I lived in one place for so long or known a place so well. It was my place, my home.

Wherever we live, every season has a unique gift, a smell, a presence of its own. Each flower, tree, bird, or cloud. What would life be without all this beauty freely given from the earth? The full light of the moon is enchanting, mesmerizing, dazzling at times. Then, it begins to wane and reminds us that nothing lasts. Nothing stays. It's the clinging that hurts, the attachment to wanting things to remain the same when they never will. Aspen trees bud out in the spring, leaf into green, turn golden and drop off. There is a continuous cycle of birth, life, death, decay.

Nature is reassuring in its predictability. We know what to expect. We think we know what's coming - until we don't. Life is unpredictable. Best-laid plans fall through. Hopes are dashed. Expectations go unfulfilled. When I'm upset, anxious, or grieving if I can, I go outside, go for a walk and spend time in nature because it grounds me, soothes me, and gives me joy.

We move in and out of the big picture and the minutiae of life. As we do, the sense of place changes and evolves. Place, defined as to know or keep one's place, to recognize one's position or rank, especially if inferior, and behave or act accordingly, is the least helpful, most narrow definition of place. Place can be a residence or dwelling, a region or area.

A woman's place, rank, position, or status, is still undervalued and underpaid.

There are frightening places for women to be.

A woman's place is hauling water in a large jug on her head for kilometers. Building a fire for a meager meal.

A woman's place is the crowd outside of a school waiting for news about her child. Worried about gun violence. Scared of the police.

A woman's place is in the home wondering whether or not her partner will kill her this time.

A woman's place is selling her body for food, drugs or alcohol.

What if we shift the paradigm? Create a celebratory vision of feminine nature?

A woman's place is rooted in the earth. In the woods. By the sea. At the top of a mountain. In the grasslands. Gazing up at the sky, the stars, the moon.

A woman's place is in a circle with other women holding hands in support and solidarity. Drumming in a circle. Dancing with her sisters.

A woman's place is deep inside her heart and soul.

A woman's place is on the wings of a bird. On the hoof of an elk. A wolf's paw. A bear's tooth. The roar of a lioness.

How would you describe your place as a woman in the world?

SING A SONG OF POWER

It's been ten years since I shed menstrual blood. I have a menstrual story. It's an ordinary one for an American woman born in the 1950s. There was no rite of passage, no welcoming circle of women, no red tent. There was embarrassment, inconvenience, and discomfort.

For many years I was out of touch with my own cyclical nature. I wasn't paying attention. It wasn't that I didn't know, I didn't tune in.

I was able to conceive and bear two healthy girls. Again, they had no rite of passage when they got their periods, no welcoming circle of women. They probably would have killed me if I'd tried. I feel regret that I didn't do better. I wish I had had a song to sing to them.

Even though the blood mysteries are powerful, there's been much shame around menstruation. Centuries ago women knew their songs. I'm happy that modern women are bringing ancient knowledge forward and into consciousness again.

There's some confusion about menopause. It's defined medically as occurring 12 months after the last menstrual period and marks the end of menstrual cycles. Peri-menopause is where The Change actually begins to occur. Peri-menopause is like going through puberty backward and can last for years. The physical symptoms are unpredictable and unnerving.

Even though It's a relief not to be plagued by erratic hormonal mood swings, there is also a sense of loss. I

104

miss the wild animal feeling of bleeding, the incredible potential of conception, and the energetic ebb and flow contained within my body.

If this is the blood that transforms us, then what happens when we no longer bleed? We strengthen our inner power. We become Wise Women. We assess our lives and continue to move forward. We must connect with the moon and her light, her ebb and flow, in order to continue our rhythmic cycles of energy.

Post-menopausal women hold within them all aspects of life. We contain the life of a maiden, the young girl whose life is stretching out endlessly before her. We hold within us the life of a mother and the creations that have been brought forth, birthed in blood, sweat and tears. We bear witness to the wisdom of the crone. Each life stage is a transformation, a metamorphosis, and yet we are the same person. We contain the whole of our existence.

Transformation happens slowly over time, usually in small increments, until there is a pivotal moment of surprise when we look in the mirror and ask, "Who am I now?" With the post-menopausal stage of life, comes a time for turning inward. As our estrogen supplies decrease, we become less concerned about taking care of others. We gain a new sense of enthusiasm, sometimes referred to as Post-Menopausal Zest. It's a vital time for discovering lost dreams and seeking new directions.

There are also fears: the fear of aging, the loss of physical and mental abilities, the fear of losing loved ones, the fear of illness or death. Yet, this is all a part of life. Tragedy can strike suddenly at any time, at any age. Therefore, learn to confront your fears now. Learn how to let go, to surrender, and to accept life as it is. These skills will serve you well now and into the future.

Pay attention to what sustains you. When you're in the midst of a busy life, it's hard to remember that, "This too shall pass." It feels like there is never enough time to take care of everyone else much less yourself. Make the time and space for what you need.

My blood power is in my life as I live it today. My creative and spiritual energies are growing as my physical abilities diminish a little at a time. I'm filled with enthusiasm, inner vitality, and curiosity. Aging becomes a spiritual practice as I adapt to change, appreciate what I've learned, and live with purpose.

What song of power will I sing at the end of my life?

The one I sing every day.

Written for Jackie Hayes' blog.

In the northern hemisphere, the days are getting shorter. We are beginning the annual descent towards the longest night of the year. The Crone whispers, "Take my hand. Come with me into the darkness. Do not be afraid."

The Crone is a post-menopausal woman. In the long ago past, it was believed that women became wise when they no longer shed the lunar "wise blood" but kept it within. The word hag, defined as an ugly old woman, especially a vicious or malicious one, usually brings up feelings of revulsion. Yet, hag originally meant "Holy Woman," queen of the dead, incarnate on earth.

Where are wise, holy women in our society today?

Wild women have been called corrupt, depraved, immoral, sinful, wanton, and wicked. They live in a state of nature, not tamed or domesticated. They are unruly, ungovernable, visionary, savage, and ferocious. These labels teach us to fear our power and deny our wisdom.

Following the Crone, I step into my cone of power as a mature woman and call upon my inner strength and courage. Raising my arms to the moon, I stand with bare feet on the cool, damp earth. I draw down the silvery light to infuse myself with power. I am both the ground and the sky. I am the warp and the weft of the tapestry of my life.

The ancient goddesses started calling me over thirty years ago. Awakened with curiosity, I read volumes of stories about the Goddess of 10,000 names. I learned about my feminine connection to the cycles of the moon. My dear friend, Kathryn, and I formed a small sisterhood, a tiny tribe of two. We desperately sought our deepest selves out of a strong desire to reclaim our personal power. Our wild hearts were drawn to ceremonies that connected us to the sacred cycles of nature. Although it was unusual at that time, Kathryn and I also lifted weights and studied martial arts together. We were Amazons, Wild Women Warriors.

We continued to read voraciously and talked endlessly about women's spiritual practices. Kathryn created a sacred space in her basement, *The Red Room*, painting it entirely dark red. The dark red color represented our return to the sacred womb of creation from which we all begin our journey into this life. We had many magical moments sharing our thoughts, hopes, and feelings, as we became everlasting Moon Sisters.

It's a little difficult to convey exactly what it was like to be on the brink of discovery all those years ago. Then, mainstream ears misunderstood the word "goddess." Now, bookshelves are crammed with volumes written about women's spirituality. It's almost impossible to choose from the unlimited Tarot decks, Oracle decks, and Angel cards. It's not unusual to read women online discussing all things related to the goddess and the moon, but it wasn't always that way.

The Wheel of Life turns again and again.

Having made the springtime journey from maiden, into and through the summer of motherhood, I'm beginning my descent into the Shadow Lands, now in the autumn of my life. There have been times when I was cracked apart by pain and sorrow during dark winters of my soul, but the experience of aging is a different kind of journey. There is no return to springtime.

The crone stage and the knowledge of the ancient ones have been obliterated by our youth-worshipping culture, yet within us is a connection to the Divine Dark. We need compassionate and loving discussions about our attitudes toward aging. We must learn how to celebrate the depths of wisdom that come from living a long time.

Awaken with curiosity! Ancient goddess wisdom is not lost. There is an iridescent rainbow of goddesses that represents courage, strength, and healing for all of us. We can collect powerful symbols and images that will guide us back to our truest selves.

If we answer the Crone's whisper, She will guide us through our darkest nights. Claim the unruly and ferocious wisdom of the Elders, acknowledge their insight, and greet them without fear or aversion. If we do, we will become the Wise, Holy Women we seek to know and understand.

**May you be restored to wholeness
in the darkness
of the waning light.**

Originally written for Roots of She.

ANCIENT WISDOM FOR MODERN TIMES

Once upon a time I lived in a tiny duplex on a street nicknamed "Baltic Avenue." My mattress rested on a floor that sloped towards the bathroom. Every morning I stumbled downhill towards the toilet. My bedroom was also a magical place. Crystals hung in the eastern window, illuminating the room with rainbows as the sun rose. Posters of Pegasus decorated the walls.

Enchanted by the image of a magical white horse with wings, I collected pictures and statues of Pegasus for years. I never considered the roots of Pegasus' story until recently. I'm more curious now about his origins than I was those many years ago. My search for knowledge provided surprising and relevant information that I wish I had known sooner.

Pegasus is a symbol of spiritual elevation, transformation and transcendence. I always knew that Pegasus was born out of Medusa's blood but I didn't know the entire story. I followed that trail of blood towards a richer, deeper understanding of feminine power. When I read Barbara Walker's *Women's Encyclopedia of Myths and Secrets*, I discovered a complex and more meaningful narrative. Long ago Medusa was the serpent-goddess of the Libyan Amazon. She represented female wisdom as the destroyer aspect of the Triple Goddess, Virgin-Mother-Crone. She was similar to Kali Ma, the Hindu Triple Goddess of creation, preservation and destruction.

A Gorgon was a monstrous feminine creature within the complicated pantheon of Greek gods and

110

goddesses. Her face would turn anyone who laid eyes upon it to stone. Gorgons were hideous beings with impenetrable scales, hair of living snakes, hands made of brass and sharp fangs. They guarded the entrance to the underworld. A stone head or picture of a Gorgon was often placed or drawn on temples to avert the dark forces of evil. Medusa was one such Gorgon.

Medusa embodied the principle of medha, the Indo-European root word for female wisdom. Pegasus was named for the Pegae, water priestesses who tended the sacred spring of Pirene in Corinth, Greece. Pegasus represented divine inspiration. His crescent moon-shaped hoof stamped the ground and dug the Hippocrene (Horse-Well), a spring of poetic inspiration on Mount Helicon, the home of the Muses.

In a late version of the Medusa myth, related by the Roman poet Ovid (Metamorphoses 4.770), Medusa is a ravishingly beautiful maiden, "the jealous aspiration of many suitors." Poseidon rapes Medusa in Athena's temple. The enraged Athena transforms Medusa's beautiful hair into serpents and makes her face so terrible to behold that the mere sight of it turns onlookers to stone.

King Polydectes, the ruler of Seriphos, enters the story. He wants to marry Danaë, the only child of the king of Argos; however, her son, Perseus, doesn't approve. In an effort to get rid of Perseus, the king sends him to fetch Medusa's head, expecting him to die. Athena assists Perseus by giving him a mirrored shield. He views Medusa's reflection in the shield and cuts off her head. Immediately, Pegasus springs from Medusa's blood.

This latter version of the story is disturbing in that Medusa is blamed and punished by Athena even though she is Poseidon's victim. In another twist, Athena co-opts Medusa's power by placing Medusa's face upon her shield. Yet, after many millennia, Medusa remains a compelling symbol of wild feminine power. Paradoxically, she is a dangerous, unruly woman who invokes fear and she is also a potent image of inner strength for women.

Wild women are condemned as corrupt, depraved, immoral, sinful, wanton, and wicked. Women who live in a state of nature, not tamed or domesticated, are unruly, ungovernable, visionary, savage and ferocious. These derogatory labels teach us to fear each other, our power, and to deny our inner wisdom. Strong-willed women are demonized in the patriarchal system and socialized to behave.

American historian Laurel Thatcher Ulrich pointed out that, "Well behaved women seldom make history." She lamented the fact that women who made positive impacts on society have been consistently overlooked in general education. We've been well-trained to behave, to stay in our place.

I have my own well-behaved past. In my family of origin, I was taught to be passive, compliant, and pleasing. I barely knew my own truth, and if I did, I was afraid to speak it. Feelings were never expressed. I wasn't provided any feminine models of wisdom or power.

When I was in graduate school, I took a life-altering class, Women's Issues. It was the equivalent of a 1970's consciousness-raising group. I learned about the oppression of women and the suppression of feminine power throughout the ages. For centuries, women have been schooled to disconnect from their ancient ways of knowing about their bodies, their intuition and the natural world with all its magic and mystery. Stories about wild women certainly weren't taught in my schools or church. These institutions continue to sustain patriarchal propaganda about the dominance of men and the subservience of women. Aversion and fear towards our own menstrual blood, aging, and death are considered normal.

When it sank in how much women's history was omitted or distorted from my education, I was completely outraged. One day I went home and beat a towel around the house, screaming until I accidentally broke a lightbulb. Then, in a mad frenzy, I cleaned the entire house with all that energy.

During this same timeframe, I studied martial arts and used karate to channel my rage. I felt the need to learn how to defend myself. Filled with self-righteous indignation, I sized up men as opponents and taunted them until a man set his own limits and put his boot about an inch away from my face. I learned then to tone it down a little but the anger still roiled within me.

Patriarchal mythology distorts the feminine forces of life and nature and sets out to destroy those forces in myriad ways. Whether or not dismantling the power of the goddess and the planet was deliberate is a topic for another essay. Either way, we've been socialized to perpetuate destructive forms of power, control, and intimidation.

As women, we must nurture one another, build each other up, and educate ourselves. Ancient and modern patriarchal stories have encouraged us to feel antagonistic towards and alienated from ourselves and other women. As women, we contain deep reservoirs of intuition and life-giving power. It's important that we shift our consciousness towards support, empathy and understanding.

I've worked for over three decades to transform my rage into spiritual growth. Repeatedly, I'm called to face my darkest emotions. I continue to read voraciously in order to educate myself about the ways in which patriarchal thinking has influenced my life. My experience and wisdom grows as I age. My inner power evolves as a result of my journey through life.

Clarissa Pinkola Estes wrote, "A good deal of literature on the subject of women's power states that men are afraid of women's power. I always want to exclaim, 'Mother of God! So many women themselves are afraid of women's power.'" Divine feminine forces are vast and formidable. Not only have we been conditioned to fear our own power, sometimes we fear other women and tear them down. Women's mythology provides inspiration for a more meaningful journey into wholeness and understanding.

Long ago, it was believed that women became wise when they no longer shed the lunar "wise blood" but kept it within. Our power as women was tied to the "blood mysteries." We bleed without dying and bear children. These mysteries have been long misunderstood and vilified. Each stage of our development, from maiden to mother then crone, has its own significance. The fear of aging is rampant in western society. As a post-menopausal woman, I can't help but notice how aging is viewed as repugnant. Aging is seen as pathology and treated like a disease. Women are terrified of turning into "hags" when, in fact, female power grows with age.

Hag originally meant "holy woman," queen of the dead, incarnate on earth. The famous Byzantine structure in Istanbul, Hagia Sophia, translates as holy wisdom. Historically, a hag has no male form or counterpart. She is a diviner, a soothsayer, a woman of prophetic and oracular powers.

The hedge was once considered the boundary between the "civilized" world and the wild keepers of primal mysteries. The Hag is She Who Straddles the Hedge. Today, the word hag is defined as an ugly old woman, especially a vicious or malicious one. Sadly, now the hag brings up feelings of revulsion instead of reverence.

Medusa was fearsome. She represented Death and to see her face was to die; turning to stone symbolized dying and becoming a funerary statue. Pegasus, born from her magical blood, led me to her. Medusa is a Holy Hag, not a monster. She is a Wise Woman and a Guardian of the Divine Dark. I feel a strong affinity with Medusa and compassion for her story. Her snakes are not evil. They are a symbol of transformation. She doesn't fear her divine power. She is a timeless guardian of magic and healing. Medusa is a protector of women's wisdom, a protector we need now more than ever. I long for her potent, transformative energy to enter our world.

I'm integrating Medusa as a wild and powerful part of myself. If we, as ferocious women, learn to embrace our wild nature and capacity for the full range of emotions - if we don't turn away - we can dismantle patriarchal conditioning. Inner feminine power grows from the Divine Dark, the Underworld, where our earthy parts of self remain until we bring them to the light of day.

Vicki Noble, creator of the *Motherpeace Tarot Deck*, states that to "break free of the chains that bind us to old habit patterns and stuck ways of thinking requires an Amazon consciousness, a Medusa-like focus on victory." Behaviors and attitudes of the past are no longer valid for us. We need to courageously speak up for ourselves and each other.

Medusa encourages us to transform ourselves, to grow spiritually and offers Pegasus as a symbol of transcendence. Medusa invites us to cope with our fear, terror and rage, to confront our resistance to aging, and to challenge the negative thinking about our wild feminine nature. The question is, will we accept her invitation?

As we move into a new era sociologically and politically, we could be called to engage in civil disobedience. Kali Akuno, the Director of Human Rights Education at the U.S. Human Rights Network, states, "If we are serious and steadfast, we can create a clear and comprehensive message around being ungovernable." Challenged to reframe our culture, we will need Medusa-like ferocity to fight for human rights, to turn outmoded ways of thinking into stone.

Perhaps Medusa doesn't speak to you as clearly as she speaks to me. It's possible that you might need to do your own research on powerful women, goddesses and priestesses. I encourage you to find your own inner guide and symbol of feminine power. Call upon her when you feel the need for strength and assistance. She will answer you.

French feminist writer, Hélène Cixous wrote, "You only have to look at the Medusa straight on to see her. And she's not deadly. She's beautiful and she's laughing." Medusa, crowned with the snakes of transformation, wise from experience, is laughing in ecstasy, inspiring us to live a courageous, powerful existence.

Originally published in *Re-visioning Medusa: from Monster to Divine Wisdom; a girl god anthology*.

THE EDGES OF TIME (2017)

Let your life lightly dance on the edges of Time like dew on the tip of a leaf. ~ Rabindranath Tagore

I want to understand time. Yes, I can read a clock or consult the calendar, but that's not the experience of time that I'm trying to understand. The passing of time is a mystery to me. If I time a minute with a clock and watch the second hand travel around the face, it feels like a long time. If I go do something fun, the hours fly by. I can remember things that happened forty years ago like they were yesterday but often I can't remember what I actually did the day before. (That could be more of a function of memory than time, though.)

The clock is one of the oldest human inventions. People seem compelled to consistently measure intervals of time shorter than what happens naturally - the day, the lunar month, and the year. Sundials were used before the advent of mechanical clocks. Now we have concise atomic clocks that keep time based on atomic physics. The challenge for me is that tracking time more accurately still doesn't describe my experience of time.

I'd like to return to the days when the sun, the stars, and the moon were used to reckon time. Before clocks and calendars, aboriginal people used celestial events for navigation and timekeeping. They depended on the night sky. Native Americans used natural seasons and lunar cycles to mark time. The cycles of nature organized task-based labor; such as planting corn or tobacco. Most Native Americans tracked time by nights rather than by days.

Paying attention to the passing of time slows it down. Slowing down opens me up to a feeling of spaciousness that allows time for contemplation and growth. If I make the time to be still, to breathe, and to calm down, I experience peace of mind. With stillness comes awareness. I become more present. I start to appreciate the many small moments that make up the day. I experience more gratitude. These are the states of mind I want to cultivate now that I have more time.

I'm retired from my profession but I'm still affected by the outside world. Many things are happening beyond my control and it causes me anxiety about the future. In the U.S., people are busy all the time, rushing everywhere, and complaining they never have enough time. Anxiety and depression are prevalent. News and social media perpetuate an all-pervasive sense of fear. This constant state of agitation causes stress and physical problems over time.

It's a fact that things change, it's part of the fabric of life. Change is inseparable from our natural state of being. I'm growing older and my body is changing. It's an unavoidable process I can either accept or resist. My time alive is a precious gift but it sure does seem like it's all going by too fast.

ON THE THRESHOLD OF TIME (2019)

A portal connects points in time. Was I inspired by Marie Kondo videos or did planetary aspects motivate me? Mountains of boxes cluttering the guest room closet pushed me over the edge. I reached the point of zero tolerance and pulled out the first box.

A box of memories filled with pictures, letters, cards, books, small mementos. More boxes. A keychain from a trip to the Big Apple. My oldest daughter's Big Bird toy. Happy Mother's Day drawings. Souvenirs and tickets from foreign countries. Trash. Recycling. Books. Journals.

Each memento was a portal to another time, a different lived experience, sometimes forgotten or laid aside. Momentum accelerated (perhaps a bit of frenzy occurred) until four closets and two rooms were decluttered and reorganized in epic fashion. It was exhausting, rewarding and ultimately liberating.

A friend shared a bit of wisdom yesterday, "Look around, where you are, there you are!" Here I am indeed. And what a place it is to be.

Soon I'll be officially married for half of my life. In an interesting game of numbers, I'll be 66 in April and married for 33 years. I don't know why this amuses me but it does.

I never imagined living in Wyoming, either. But here I am. Renewed.

And, I have this website, a creative evolution, a portal of time and space where you can peek in and see me.

A me produced by an electronic keyboard, a twinkling amalgam of thoughts and photons.

When you read this I won't be here in this space any more.

Note: My website, LoranHills.com, is also gone now.

SLOWING DOWN TIME

Time appears to go by so quickly. We ask each other, "Where does the time go?" or "How does the time go by so fast?"

How do we slow time down? How do we savor life? How do we get to the end of our lives and say, "That was time well spent."

We need to spend time in the Still Point, that sacred place of power and mystery within us, our center. It's the quiet eye of the hurricane. This is a daily practice, not a one-time fix.

Within the maelstrom of life, the still point is quiet. We can choose what we want to cultivate: expansiveness, love, and joy or regret and bitterness. Experiment with different methods to help slow down and focus your awareness. Instead of feeling fear or resistance, focus on developing a sense of well-being. Practice enjoying life and feeling grateful so that it becomes a regular habit. It helps to pay attention to our emotional patterns, our physical senses, and nature.

Paying attention generates awareness and helps us become fully present. By paying attention to the passing of time, we slow time down. Slowing down opens us up to a feeling of spaciousness that in turn allows time for contemplation and growth. Time is not an enemy, it's a precious gift.

Get comfortable and right now, take a deep breath.

Focus on being fully present.

Now.

It's gone.

Deep breath.

Another.

Now.

It's gone.

Breathe.

How long can you sit still and just breathe? It's ok to start with 30 seconds. Just observe what happens.

Can you go without your TV, radio, phone or computer for a short period of time? What do you do when your mind starts to race? What do you reach for first? Just take note without judgement.

Are you thinking about what to cook for dinner? Or that you have to pick up the kids or take them somewhere? That you need to check your email?

Sit another minute.

Then another.

If this causes anxiety or a trauma response, that's ok too. Just observe the moment it begins without judging and rest.

If you have a clock with a second hand, watch it move around the dial.

It. Takes. A. Long. Time.

It's our mind that's in a rush. Our ego pushes us to succeed, to move, to react. Don't judge yourself for having thoughts. It's your mind's job to think. Don't be concerned when you notice your "monkey mind." It's a positive sign that you're becoming more aware.

Where is your center, your Still Point? Is it a place, a feeling? Can you draw it? Take a picture? Describe what it feels like to be still. Write about what happens when you try.

Think of a lake. The water is still. It looks like glass. What do you see reflected in it?

If you can, stand outside and get grounded. Hug a tree. Sit in the grass. Look up at the sky. Listen to the birds. Nature can teach you stillness.

Many Moondays ago, I lived in Pocatello, Idaho, in a little cottage on a secluded alley. There was just enough room for me, my big dog Tess and my marvelous cat, Byrd. The house was situated on a little wild patch in the middle of the city. The magical yard was overgrown and the fence was covered in greenery.

I could also easily walk up to the top of Red Hill from there. My friend, Kathryn, and I would take Tess with us at night and gaze out at the lights. Sometimes we talked about our past lives, like when we were priestesses in Greece. It was easy to do. Idaho State University had placed four pillars up there, giving it the feel of an ancient ruin.

One day I came home to find someone hacking my yard down. Shocked, I asked, "What are you doing?" The hired man said he was cleaning up the yard. He destroyed it and left it barren. At that moment, I had a profound epiphany. Suddenly I deeply felt the devastation perpetrated by white settlers in America. Without regard for people, animals, or forests, they decimated a way of life. They greedily took everything for themselves.

Since then, and it's been many years, I've felt uneasy with manicured yards and formal gardens. They feel alien to me. I don't like trimming and pruning vegetation. It gets harder and harder every year to do it. I want to let my yard turn into forest again.

I feel so connected to Mother Earth. I want to see her waters clean and lands robed in green always. I wish we took better care of Her. Of all the battles raging now, the one I feel most ferocious about is the fight for our environment.

Instead of sticking my head in the sand, I want to blow iridescent love bubbles. I choose to take my magic bubble wand and dip it into a charmed elixir made of the scent of pine, a sunny day, flowers bursting open covered in bees. Mix in the scent of sage, an ocean breeze, wood burning on the hearth, and rich black soil. Add a full belly, hot running water, and warm embraces.

Blowing love bubbles out into the universe, like a prayer flag sending prayers, mends my broken heart for a moment. I know how things are. I've raged against it all but as the wheel turns, leaves fly off the trees, and days shorten, I turn in towards what's whole and beautiful.

STILLNESSE (2020)

at the still point, there the dance is ~ T. S. Elliott

The word stillness comes from the Middle English, stillnesse for tranquility, peace, security.

It's paradoxical to think of dancing in stillness, but isn't that what many of us are doing now? (Note: Written during Covid lockdown.)

It's been a month of social isolation for me, my husband, and two dogs. Our retired lifestyle was already quiet. After we moved to Wyoming, we stopped hosting potlucks with our friends. Family gatherings here are on hold. It's Easter Sunday and we have six inches of new snow.

Our society isn't used to being still, stillness needs to be cultivated or scheduled. It's possible to be still but not calm. Emotions and feelings rise up, internal dialogue is noisy, and agitation continues. It takes practice and those of us who are healthy or don't have a houseful of hungry children have the opportunity to practice now. Not everyone is getting a privileged time out. And, in spite of our collective stillness, there isn't a feeling of security.

I like this old word, stillnesse. Shakespeare used it to mean restraint, sobriety, quietness of behavio(u)r. We are restraining ourselves socially but perhaps not so much on social media. There are too many theories, ideas, facts, pseudo-facts, and predictions. Media runs amuck with fear-mongering.

Nobody really knows what the future holds. We never did but it looks different now than it did even a month ago. I reduced the amount of news and posts I was consuming just to maintain some level of sanity.

The challenge is staying out of fear and remaining in today, being present in the moment. There are articles galore about how or when or if we can return to some state of normalcy. They cause me to become more anxious and worry about all the what if's.

I'm grateful that I have coping skills, abilities I've been practicing for a long time. Sobriety. Meditation. Mindfulness. Lovingkindness. Creativity. I'm writing, drumming, painting, walking when the weather is nice. I also binge-watch Netflix and Hulu. I'm human.

What are your thoughts about stillnesse? What do you wish you could do?

One thing for sure – we're all in this together. Globally. In the future, I'd like to see humans return to a deeper sense of community with more willingness to help each other. We need to consume fewer natural resources and give back to the planet in the spirit of reciprocity. It's going to take a huge shift in consciousness.

Stillnesse could be a new, quieter way of life that allows for more reflection and less noise.

Why not?

At this still point in time, anything is possible.

A SPIRAL JOURNEY THROUGH THE SEASONS OF MY PLACE

In all seasons, in all directions, I walk the land. I become naturalized to the land.

I raise my arms and greet the east:

In my youth, I dreamed of living in the country. Eventually, my dream came true. My husband and I live on twenty acres in the alpine desert of northeastern Utah. Surrounded by sagebrush, cedars, and juniper trees, our house sits at 6800' (2072m). Cactus, sego lilies, and Indian paintbrush bloom in the spring. The Uintah (you-in-tah) mountain range is the only one in the US that runs east–west.

Today I walked east on a gravel road to the mailbox. Brigid's Day is in the past but it's not yet Spring Equinox. The days are getting longer.

Spring weather is unpredictable. "If you don't like it, wait five minutes." We can experience snow, rain, sun, and hail all in one day.

My two children were young maidens when we moved here and, although they could roam free, they often preferred to play inside. I never understood this. As a city kid, I longed to play outside in the woods.

I raise my arms and greet the south:

Castle Cove is magical. It's a stunning blend of rock formations and pine trees. Fog and snowstorms arrive over the top of the mountain and swirl around the rocks. The play between sun and clouds, weather and terrain is enchanting.

We live at the end of a dead-end road. Visitors from the city comment on how quiet it is. Today I heard the wind and the birds.

Summer weather is dry, windy, and hot, but not unbearably so. Sometimes there are large and dangerous fires.

As teenagers, my daughters couldn't easily sneak in and out of the house. They couldn't get cell service then either. It was a good thing.

I raise my arms and greet the west:

Pine Ridge is covered in Ponderosa pines; they are large, old, magnificent trees. One of them is my special friend. I visit when I can but it's a steep, treacherous climb up. After a back injury last year, I climbed down from the road to visit instead but it wasn't the same. It's a sacred pilgrimage.

There is a two-hour hike from the house to a cow pond at the bottom of Sawtooth Ridge where once I saw a coyote. We frequently hear them at night. I've seen fox too. The jackrabbit and cottontail populations ebb and flow.

Fall is usually the most beautiful season of the year with its balmy days and chilly nights.

My children are in college and my nest is empty now except for the holidays and summer.

I raise my arms and greet the north:

Dry Fork Canyon is well known to tourists who travel the Red Cloud Loop Road to behold the sandstone cliffs and wildlife. I've traveled to many exotic places in the world, but the Flume Trail remains one of my favorite places to hike. Every excursion on the trail is unique to the time of day and season.

Winter can be harsh, extremely cold, and filled with snowy days. It lasts a long time; sometimes it feels eternal. Although it's not good for the water table, this winter has been quite mild.

We live with animals, both wild and domestic. Every evening a flock of wild turkeys peck and scratch under our bird feeders looking for seeds before they roost at night in the cottonwood trees. Deer raid the bird feeders too and eat my columbines and daylilies. Blue jays hop into the duck coop looking for scratch. Occasionally, in winter, a goshawk will come down from the pines and scout its prey.

Driving home one night a mountain lion crossed the road in front of me. I was so thrilled I almost stopped breathing. Some time ago a moose met me on the Flume Trail. I've seen traces of bear on the trail too. Our llamas sound their alarm when there are intruders. The dogs are more friendly when they greet new arrivals. Skunks, raccoons, and magpies enjoy the cat food.

The circle is cast.

I grew up on the east coast where it's congested with people and vegetation. When I first moved "out west," the terrain was vast beyond my visual comprehension. Now I adore the open space.

Little Mountain is red in color and sits above the Dry Fork Cemetery, an old settlement graveyard. Although it's not groomed, there are a lot of quirky decorations, stone benches, and well-seasoned headstones. I felt inexplicably happy when I bought my burial plot a few years ago.

With camera in hand, I've increased my awareness of minute changes in light and season. My connection to the Earth nourishes my spirit daily. I have become naturalized to this land that I love wholeheartedly.

The circle is open but not broken.

Note: In *Braiding Sweet Grass*, Robin Wall Kemmerer addresses the problems around white appropriation from those who are native to land in the United States. She suggests that those who are not native can become "naturalized." I changed my vocabulary accordingly after this was posted on Joanna Powell Colbert's website years ago.

GROWING ROOTS (2018)

The moment my husband announced he wanted to move back home to Wyoming, I immediately felt like an uprooted plant. We lived in Utah for 24 years, built a dream home on 20 acres in a stunning, desert alpine landscape, and raised our daughters in a place with room to roam. Sandstone cliffs changed with the light and season on our drive up and down the canyon. It was the first time in my life I felt rooted to a place.

In *Braiding Sweetgrass*, Robin Wall Kemmerer writes about becoming "naturalized" to a place, like an immigrant who becomes a new citizen. As a non-indigenous person, I wasn't native to the land, but I learned to love it and connect with it as I walked for miles in every direction - up Deep Creek, over to Sawtooth Mountain, on the Flume Trail. I can still see and feel it in my mind's eye.

I walked three or four times a week with my dear friend and neighbor, Kaye, on the Flume Trail. The trail was just a five-minute drive away. We loved the scenery as well as our time together talking about everything under the sun. One morning, after a big rainstorm the night before, we headed up the trail. It was twilight in the canyon, still chilly. As the sun rose over the sandstone canyon walls, everything, the trees, the grass, and the rocks, began to glisten. In a matter of moments, we were standing in a magical world of sparkling light. We stopped walking and stood in total awe, surrounded by dazzling beauty.

The next day, I brought my camera but the magic was gone. Such numinous moments of awareness are fleeting. I will never forget that breathtaking moment of enchantment when we felt connected to the magical light of the natural world.

After we moved, I was indeed uprooted. We landed here in Wyoming four years ago on May 10. I'm a transplant once again. I grew up in Virginia, outside of Washington, D.C. I was a city kid without experience in the natural world. After forty-one years of living in the west, I now prefer open spaces, mountains, wildlife, hiking, and camping more than I enjoy a visit to the city.

With enormous gratitude, I found a trail ten minutes from my house where I walk and, once again, connect deeply with the natural world. It calms me and lifts my heart. There's still snow up there so I'm waiting for the opportunity to return. Winter seemed to go on forever but finally, the grass is greening up and daffodils are blooming. Today we saw the first tulips.

Mother Earth gives everything to us. We have taken from her for far too long. Now we're seeing the devastating consequences of long-term abuse. Will we be able to turn the tide? The jury is out at the moment. For me, in an effort not to appropriate traditions that don't belong to me, but out of a desire to celebrate the land, our Earth, her gifts, I turn to my ancestral roots - English, French, Swiss, and Austrian. There is a rich pagan history beneath the tedious accounts of wars. I've celebrated the Celtic Wheel with its cycles of seasons and related festivals for decades.

In the northern hemisphere, May 1 is Beltane, May Day, the essence of new growth and fertility. The wheel of life turns round and round. This May I feel more rooted than I did four years ago and for that I'm grateful. I'm learning to love this land.

We are all citizens of this planet. I desperately wish that everyone could feel what I feel when I see sandhill cranes, geese, hawks, and eagles fly overhead. I feel so much joy watching red-winged blackbirds, black-capped chickadees, and finches at my bird feeders. Meadowlark songs cheer me throughout the day. My heart lifts at the sight of gently curling green leaves and bursts wide open when trees blossom. No matter where I am, I connect with the natural world.

Spending time connecting to the natural world and its cycles is becoming more and more rare. There is even a diagnosis of Nature Deficit Disorder. Although this disorder is not recognized by the medical community, it is alarming that increasing numbers of children don't know how to play outside. City life is not necessarily conducive to paying attention to nature. As a society, we've grown sedentary and dependent on our electronic devices.

Time in nature helps reduce depression and improve mental health and well-being according to a study by the University of Essex. Walking in a natural setting is good for the physical heart and our emotional heart. It helps us become more mindful and meditative.

Our gratitude and appreciation of life grows as we accumulate many small moments of stillness and eternal beauty. These can be quite simple, ordinary moments. As you practice, your awareness will increase. Joy and peace of mind will grow.

HOME IS….. (2019)

Home is memories of meals, holidays, celebrations.

Home is feelings of belonging and estrangement.

Home is not always where the heart is, nor is it where one lives.

There was a brick house with faded white paint on Edgewood Terrace that used to be my home. I can't remember the color of the window shutters now. I do remember the large oak tree that lived outside my bedroom window. That tree provided memorable leaf piles for raking and jumping in with delight.

It was a large house with space enough for everyone to spend time in separate rooms. It was not a warm house. Not because of the radiators that banged when they turned on or the single pane windows or poor insulation.

I lived in that house for six years with my family and thought of it as home for a long time.

College dorm rooms and apartments with roommates weren't home.

Even the house I bought with my first husband didn't feel like home. We moved from Virginia to Idaho, a huge culture shock.

Does that mean home is what's outside, too? The neighborhood? The city? The home state?

The answer to this riddle is in the one place I truly called home. The one I had, the one I left behind. Nostalgic because I can't return.

Castle Cove.

I remember standing on the land, looking at the red rock formations, and saying, "This is a slice of heaven."

We hired Charlie Parker to build our "dream home." It's a myth. We came close to getting what we wanted once we picked out an affordable plan and scaled our purchases to fit the budget. We moved into a beautiful brand new house with brand-new appliances, brand-new paint, and brand-new fixtures. When we moved out it was listed as an older home.

Our girls grew up in a place I always dreamed of as a kid, a place with room to roam outside. I was the one who roamed the most. I walked everywhere with our dogs, up the Cove, over to Sawmill pond, hiked the Flume Trail and Pine Ridge.

I cast magical circles to the four directions in all seasons, a solitary practitioner. I paid attention to the moon and sun rising and setting, listened to coyotes, allowed deer to eat my flowers and birdseed. Twenty acres at the end of a dead-end road, an alpine desert filled with cedar, junipers, and sagebrush. My home. I became naturalized to the land over time.

I bought a plot in Dry Fork Cemetery. Part of my Croning Ceremony was spent lying on the ground there, waiting for the dawn. I wish I hadn't sold it. We lived in Castle Cove for many years. I knew the road home – drove it in a whiteout because it was familiar, part of a routine. Like feeding llamas in the snow, shoveling a path to their shed, running the snowblower, hauling in firewood, tending the garden.

Home is more than knowing where to find the light switches in the dark.

ILLUMINATING SPIRITUAL PRACTICE

My life's journey is a spiral path. Like you, I travel through the seasons and the cycles of the sun and moon. My wisdom emerges from integrating life's lessons. I'm grateful to have the opportunity to share what I've learned with you.

Sometimes life is marvelous and magical. Sometimes it's hard. Some days are heartbreakingly beautiful and poignant. There are infinite circumstances and reactions.

Endlessly curious, I'm always asking questions, seeking knowledge, and studying new things. Maybe you're curious too. Perhaps you're curious about your truest self. It may be that you need help coping with life's ups and downs. I have ideas and suggestions.

In 2012 I compiled and edited <u>Twelve Sessions of Illuminating Spiritual Practice</u>. The course appeared on my blog during the summer. Eventually, it was edited into a downloadable pdf. It's updated here, in 2023, brimming with ideas and techniques to help you explore your spiritual path and deepen your spiritual practices.

PART ONE: SPIRITUAL EXCAVATION

What does spirituality mean to you? I believe it's a practice of depth that connects me to all that is. It's permission to have a relationship with God, Creator, Source, or a Higher Power of my own understanding. My spiritual path has grown and changed dramatically over the years. Spiritual growth isn't linear. It can be a spiral shape or a meandering trail. There may be hills and valleys, dark caves, or bright moons. Each path is unique.

Religious traditions have evolved through time to help us understand the world and our place in it. They contain doctrine, rules for conduct, and a sense of community. Religions can provide a comfortable, familiar structure.

Spiritual wellness can be defined as experiencing harmony between what lies inside you and the forces that influence you from the outside. Your ability to be resilient in the face of challenges is a good indicator of your spiritual health. A strong practice will get you through difficult times and enhance your feelings of joy and gratitude in good times. An attitude of curiosity and playful exploration will help you excavate old patterns and behaviors so that you can create healthier ways of being in the world.

Change is a part of life. It is inevitable and completely unavoidable. We create new cells all the time, we change chronologically, relationships change, people are born and they die. Yet we cling to outmoded behaviors and belief systems. Letting go becomes necessary to move forward.

Wellness requires answering hard questions. Sometimes those answers don't arrive readily. It takes time and patience to explore new realms, new ways of thinking. Let's begin by exploring your personal history of spiritual practices.

Creating a Spiritual Timeline

The spiritual timeline is a useful tool for gaining perspective on your spiritual history. It's a way for you to evaluate how you were raised, how you've evolved and changed over time and to figure out where you are now.

You can't know where you're going unless you know where you are!

To begin, get a piece of paper and something to write with. If you are creative and would like to collage, paint, draw, or otherwise embellish your timeline, then please do. Otherwise, you can keep it simple and speak into your phone. If you have a journal, you can use that. Or, you can dedicate a new journal specifically to spiritual practice. It can be handy to have all your spiritual thoughts, favorite quotes, and prayers in one notebook.

Turn your page horizontally and draw a line across it. On the left side of the page, write the year of your birth above the line. Below the line write a description of the religious orientation of the family you grew up in, if you have one.

For example, I was baptized into the Episcopal Church. We attended church regularly as a family. I was confirmed at age 12 and wore a white dress for my first communion from the local Archbishop.

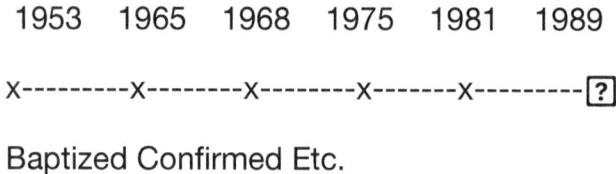

1953   1965   1968   1975   1981   1989

X---------X--------X--------X-------X---------?

Baptized Confirmed Etc.

Spend some time thinking about what you were taught and what you learned as a child about religion, if anything. Not having a faith or practice as a child can affect you as well. Make notes below the line regarding your religious origins. If memories and feelings you had as a child arise and you wish to explore those further, write about them on a separate page or in your journal.

Return to the line and make an X or a short vertical line and mark the age or year when you first started asking Big Questions like, "Why am I here? What does it all mean? Where is my place in the world?" Perhaps you stopped going to church or experienced some spiritual change. Mark that and make notes about that time period. Again, return to the line and mark the next significant stage in your spiritual growth.

I was 15 when I started to consider the size of the universe and realized that I was a very small part of it. I really wondered what it was all about but I didn't talk to anyone about it. I felt scared and confused.

As a flower child of the early 70s, I was influenced by the culture and politics of the times. I enjoyed reading the mystical Carlos Castaneda books that were very popular. I started to explore new realms of thought in college, in class, and outside of class. My mind expanded in different directions and interesting ways from 18 to 22. I experimented with a lot of new behaviors and drugs during this time.

When I was 22, my first love died unexpectedly. As a result, I became much more interested in spirituality and life after death. It was 1975 so there wasn't a lot of information available. I read Edgar Cayce books and whatever else I could get my hands on. I was devastated and lost, emotionally and spiritually. My consumption of drugs and alcohol escalated.

At age 28 my spiritual pendulum swung drastically when I took a Women's Issues class as part of my Masters in Counseling. I learned a new perspective on religious history that ignited a rather lengthy feminist rage stage. I felt betrayed and lied to by the Episcopal Church.

I started reading the emerging female spiritual leaders of the time: Starhawk, Z Budapest, Anne Kent Rush, and Anne Wilson Schaef. I fell in love with an earth-based spirituality that inspired my life-long love of nature. I was ecstatic to discover the Goddess. For the first time in my life, a Divine image looked like me. Representation does indeed matter.

Motherhood at 35 calmed me down and grounded me in new ways. My second child was born shortly after I turned 38. For many years I was absorbed in raising my family. At age 42 I began a program of recovery that changed my life again. I set about learning the tools I needed for creating a more joyous life. I started to experience clarity of mind and serenity for the first time.

As a lifelong student dedicated to learning, and as an equally dedicated seeker, I branched off yet again. In January 2011, at age 57, I took refuge vows and became a Buddhist in the Tibetan tradition. My first teacher, Lama Thupten, told me after I took my vows that I would now be a Buddhist in all my future incarnations. Apparently, there is no turning back! This tradition offers explicit directions for experiencing peace of mind and psychological health. It is often referred to as a religion but I think of it more as a healthy psychological and spiritual practice.

In the last few years, I've discovered women in Buddhism who combine feminist thought and nature-based approaches with the more traditional Vajrayana practices. There is a male hierarchy in Buddhism that is problematic. Prominent leaders have been called out on their physical, mental, and sexual abuse of students. As with other religious institutions and teachers, we have to be discerning.

I share my own timeline for a number of reasons. It's eclectic and varied and reveals why I draw on so many different traditions and at the same time look for similarities. It also reveals how I have changed dramatically throughout my lifetime. My path has not always been as illuminated as it is now.

Now that I'm in my "Third Age," this last portion of my life is bringing together many skills and experiences that I'm excited to share with others. Also, in sharing my own timeline, I can see how much I've changed.

What I emphatically believed in my 30s isn't what I now believe at age 70. I'm finally growing wiser.

Creating your own spiritual timeline will bring you from the past into the present. When you see future spiritual developments emerging, you can jot those down as well. Be sure to make note of your feelings in each stage. Start a journal for your timeline and answer these questions, if you like.

Document people or institutions that shifted your thinking about spirituality.

What does your spiritual timeline reveal about you?

Did you stop growing somewhere along the line? Or, was there a time you started to grow and change?

Did you move away from your family traditions or incorporate them?

Did any events occur that shook your belief system?

Are you discovering new spiritual ideas that energize your inner life? What are they?

What are your current challenges spiritually?

Where do you see yourself headed in the future?

How do you connect with Spirit?

What activities help you connect to your Higher Self?

What mysteries do you wonder about?

Where do you seek answers?

How have your beliefs changed over time?

Where can you seek guidance?

PART TWO: THRESHOLD OF INNER POWER

By deepening your understanding, you strengthen your spiritual practices. In her book, *Dreaming the Dark,* Starhawk describes the concept of "power over" as domination, subjugation, and environmental destruction. She explains that the culture of estrangement is woven into our culture. The consciousness she calls "immanence" contains awareness of the interdependence of the world.

In the culture of "estrangement," one does not see oneself as part of the world. Divinity and spirit are removed from matter. How else could the brutal behaviors we see in institutions and corporations be justified? Our society is built on racist, capitalistic and patriarchal greed. It's destroying our planet.

In a culture of "immanence," power is seen as internal. Power within is generated from an awareness of the world and everything in it as alive. Thich Nhat Hanh, a well-known Buddhist monk, said that we "Inter-Are." There is no separation, no us and them. We are learning more about how alive and connected everything truly is through quantum mechanics.

Generating internal power can result in external changes. The word courage implies the presence of inner strength. It takes courage to confront "dark" feelings such as fear, anger, grief and many other demons. But it is also possible to reclaim the energy of the "life-giving dark." This is the power that comes from the womb and the earth. It is a fertile, nurturing kind of darkness.

Inner power grows from making a commitment to living a deeper life. Consciousness shapes reality through action and directed energy. To claim our inner power we must confront our difficult parts, the inner critic, the negative self-talk, and false beliefs. Growth requires deep examination of the systems that keep us feeling powerless.

When we plant seeds in the fertile, life-affirming dark, and our confidence grows one step at a time. In the beginning we need to guard our tender shoots, the little tendrils that grow from stepping beyond our comfort zones until we feel confident in full bloom.

In late 2008, I was intensely nervous about going public on the Internet. I started a blog under the pseudonym mountain mama. The first time I hit the publish button I was apprehensive. Surprised, I discovered that the world didn't end! In fact, over time, my world completely opened up. I made my first online friends. I took my first online e-course and joined my first online support group. I made more friends! Initially, it seemed strange to be sharing intimate thoughts and feelings but over time I became more comfortable. Zoom circles validate my perception that time and distance matter not. We can exist in deep communion in separate time zones and spaces.

In 2011, quitting my job and starting a business raised my fears to an entirely new level. One definition of courage is facing difficulty without fear but I believe that's inaccurate. I felt fear, a lot of it, I did every time I launched a product or posted something new, but I did it anyway. I searched deep inside myself and unearthed beliefs and values, discovered what I wanted to teach and share, and learned how to do it.

My inner power has grown slowly over time. I began a process of cultivating inner power over 30 years ago. I changed myself with intention when I realized that there were problems. I fanned little sparks of possibility until there were flames of achievement. I'm not done yet either!

Inner power comes from consistent and persistent effort over a period of time.

The courage to be arises from this kind of effort. To be who we really are is a brave act of authenticity, generating positive energy to move forward in life.

What sparks of possibility are present in your life?

Is there anything that you're afraid of right now?

How can you generate courage to move forward?

Who or what can support you?

Nine steps for handling fear

Fear is defined as a negative emotion that provokes anxiety. Fear can be useful when it protects us from a dangerous situation. Fear is a survival mechanism and operates from the "lizard" part of our brain, the amygdala. This ancient part of our brain helped us to survive in pre-historic times. It also obscures reason and intensifies emotions.

As Mark Twain so aptly put it, "I am an old man and have known a great many troubles, but most of them never happened." We generate fear in our own minds. Fear is a roadblock to personal and spiritual growth.

Our frontal lobe helps us apply logic to our fears and transform them. We are capable of mentally creating a different kind of energy that creates peace of mind. It's possible to change our behavior and generate new neural pathways in the brain.

There are many fears that create barriers to moving forward. There is fear of living, fear of dying, fear of failure, fear of success, fear of judgment, fear of the dark, fear of the unknown, the fear of fear!

What is your most prevalent fear?

I was a fearful child. Slow and uncoordinated, I was also late developing physically. I never felt like I could trust my body. The teasing from my peers caused me to feel a lot of shame, embarrassment, and consequently more fear. As an adult, I confronted my deep-seated fears when I studied martial arts for five years. Every time I passed a test to gain the next rank, I felt more confident and self-assured.

Driven by fear, there were years I spent in reckless behavior, acting out against my feelings in unhealthy ways. In retrospect, I'm appalled at some of my actions but eventually, I started to figure things out. I'm also grateful I survived.

Having children generated a new batch of fears about their vulnerability and safety and my own. I developed a healthy skill set for handling fear. Fear doesn't overwhelm me like it used to before or stop me from trying new things. Sometimes what feels like fear is excitement. Can you tell the difference?

Ultimately it was the willingness to let go of fear that moved me to explore what was going on, to soften the edges, and to open the door to releasing fear. You may wonder how this is possible.

1. Untangle the threads. Identify and acknowledge your fears. Write them down and describe your thoughts and feelings.

2. Sit with the fear for a while. Dialogue with it, draw or collage it, dance it, or sing it. Ask fear what it wants you to know. Listen to the answers. Don't push it away.

3. Ask for help from trusted friends or a therapist, if necessary.

4. Identify what you can control and what you can't control. Let go of what you can't control.

5. Practice gratitude and joy to create serenity and peace of mind. Meditate or journal about it.

6. Engage in vigorous physical exercise. Activity releases anxiety.

7. Return to your breath. Breathe deeply and slowly.

8. Return to now. Stop imaging what "could" happen.

9. Create equanimity (mental calmness) through practice.

Equanimity is a state of stability or composure arising from a deep awareness and acceptance of the present moment. It emerges from wisdom and understanding. Generate compassion for yourself and your feelings.

The nature of mind is open, expansive, and loving. Find a way that works for you to create a less fearful state of mind. Stand in the sun and let the light fill you. Sit in the dark and embrace it. Be aware of natural energy as it ebbs and flows; pay attention to the lunar cycles, the tides, and the seasons. All of life grows and ultimately dissolves. Fill yourself with love, forgiveness, harmony, and truth, and then fear will not be able to reside within you.

Letting Go

In order to live in the present, you have to be able to let go of the past and stop worrying about the future. Letting go isn't easy to do and it takes repeated effort.

Having willingness to examine your past is the first step. Have you considered being willing to let go of:

Fear

Anger

Guilt

Resentment

A story

Expectations

Attachment to outcomes

An unhealthy relationship

Addiction

All of the above?

What happens when you let go? You open up space for something new. Sometimes opening up to the unknown is terrifying, sometimes it's exhilarating. It all depends on your attitude.

Are you able to open up to new possibilities?

What possibilities are you willing to explore?

Allow time to feel your unique emotional reaction to the new space. Stay present. Every moment creates a new opportunity for letting go.

Look again at your spiritual timeline.

What did you learn by creating a spiritual timeline?

Are there beliefs that you were raised with that no longer serve you?

Are there spiritual practices you are clinging to that no longer work?

What is the payoff you receive by not changing?

Clinging is a behavior that creates suffering. Suffering can be physical, emotional, mental or spiritual.

Increase your awareness of any negative self-talk and watch your emotional reactions. You can decrease suffering with mindfulness and compassion.

> *Do you ever feel anxious, agitated, or depressed?*
>
> *Is it possible for you to make space for practices that create peace of mind?*
>
> *Are you willing to try something new or different?*

When I was living without a spiritual compass, I was frequently confused and unhappy. As I learned skills for coping and learned to accept things the way they were, my life started to improve.

> *How do you feel right now?*

Allow it to be what it is. Don't push it away or try to numb it.

> *Is there anything you are clinging to?*
>
> *Does clinging give you peace of mind? Does resistance?*
>
> *Try to remain neutral and examine the attachment – what serves you? What doesn't?*
>
> *What helps you feel lighter? What makes you feel heavier?*

Create a physical representation of an idea, feeling, or behavior that you want to release. You can write it on a piece of paper, or create a sculpture, a picture, or a collage. Whatever you create, you can release it by burying it or burning it, or setting it adrift in moving water (but be sure to avoid polluting substances).

Surrender is not defeat. Surrender makes you stronger. It's an act of humility when you give up and accept what is. Letting go leads to a state of grace, like trees in autumn letting go of their leaves.

PART THREE: THE DIVINE DARK

Why am I surprised by change? Why do I resist it? Intellectually I know nothing lasts forever or stays the same, but I want things to remain consistent. I cling to the familiar because it feels safe. Letting go feels like falling out of the nest. Fear without a spiritual anchor is alarming and uncomfortable.

Over the course of our lifetime, we develop a litany of fears, resentments, and perhaps bitterness about the way things have gone. These negative emotions can build up over time and create a lot of difficulty as we age. No one wants to look back at a life filled with regret. Compassion and forgiveness are crucial in letting go of the past.

In meditation, I remember to offer myself compassion for my fear and resistance and to replace the fear with love. In the morning, prisms often cast rainbows on my walls and ceiling. The colors and shapes enchant me. When I sit in meditation, the rainbows travel across the wall, also reminding me that time is fleeting. Nothing is permanent.

Buddhists acknowledge that death is certain, but the time of death is not. We tend to live like we have forever, but we don't. It's good practice to consider both life and death in order to discern what is important to you.

> *Are you living a life true to yourself? Is there something you might regret if you don't do it - or at least try?*

Are you working too hard and not enjoying your time? Most people on their deathbed don't say, "I wish I would have worked more."

What are your worst fears about expressing your feelings? Blocked feelings can cause emotional distress and physical side effects.

Are there friends you want to reconnect with? Are you estranged from family? Do you need to mend bridges?

Do you believe happiness is a choice?

For the longest time I didn't know that happiness is a choice. It's not about what happens to you, it's about what you tell yourself when something happens. We may not be able to control things that happen but we do have control over our response.

Western culture is not comfortable with the subject of death; however, in order to realize how sacred our life is, we need to consider our own death. This is not at all morbid or fear-based. It's a method of reinforcing the preciousness of our human existence.

Write your own obituary.

Does the thought of your own death frighten you? It's ok to feel into thoughts and feelings slowly. Gentle exploration can lessen your fears. It's not morbid to consider.

In doing this you might see more objectively what you believe you've accomplished and what remains to be done. You can be creative with it too, fill it with light and significant accomplishments, not just jobs, degrees or marital status.

You may also consider your spiritual timeline again. What kind of ceremonies would you choose for the end of your life?

> *What happiness did you choose?*
>
> *Which friends did you cherish the most?*
>
> *What did you love doing the most?*
>
> *What were your most important accomplishments? Disappointments?*

The answers to these questions can provide guidance for the way you choose to live your life today. Remember this obituary is for self-reflection and not the newspaper.

Illuminating the Dark

If I'm encouraging people to dive deeper, then I must do it as well. The longer I walk my spiritual path, the narrower it becomes. In other words, what it takes for me to stay spiritually and emotionally healthy now is more defined and critical than when I first started working on my issues.

I've been reluctant to talk about my issues in a public way, but then on the other hand, who will trust me if I'm not honest? I'm grateful to say that I was not physically or sexually abused as a child. I was taken care of physically but I suffered from emotional neglect.

I fell into the party scene quite naturally when I went to college. My pattern of avoiding and denying feelings continued with the help of sex, drugs, and rock'n'roll. My first love was physically abusive when he drank. In the early 1970s, there weren't any domestic violence programs or women's shelters. I didn't know where to turn for help. When he was sober, he was very charming, smart, and funny. He was handsome, too. It was intense and confusing on a lot of levels.

We were together off and on for four years. He died falling from some rocks in Monterey, California. I felt like the rug was pulled out from under me. There was a cannonball-sized hole in my chest. I was devastated. I used drugs and alcohol to numb my grief without success.

I married my first husband and the party continued, until it wasn't fun anymore. We had a lot of problems. When we split up I felt devastated again. Loss is loss and grief is grief. I experienced big, agonizing waves of it. I sobbed ugly tears. I felt betrayed because love didn't conquer all.

Eventually I sought help and started straightening out. I learned how to communicate, how to maintain a healthy relationship, and stopped using substances to numb my feelings. I wanted to stop feeling unhappy. I changed my life.

The dark periods of my life became gifts as I learned to open up and explore ways to change. I stopped blaming others for my problems. I quit denying and avoiding my feelings (most of the time).

I've suffered six ways from Sunday with depression, low self-esteem, body image problems, and other assorted insecurities. Partnering with men who treated me badly only mirrored my own internal negativity. With a lot of persistent effort over time, I've managed to diminish these patterns, but they continue to exist and I still get triggered.

When I suffer emotionally, it's a reminder that if I do not practice my newer and healthier habits continuously that I am in danger of getting trapped again in those dark places. Thankfully, the aging process has also helped me gain wisdom and insight into my behavior and thought processes. I'm stronger and braver now. Maturity has its benefits.

> *What periods of your life have been particularly dark? Were you able to move out of the darkness? Or, can you move out of it now?*
>
> *Can you find a gift inside? Describe it.*
>
> *What spiritual practices help prevent you from descending into darkness?*

Mindfulness Practice

Awareness practice is also called mindfulness. More formal methods of practice include scheduling a regular time for prayer or meditation, or going to church, synagogue or temple routinely. Awareness practice is less formal and ideally can be done any time, all day long.

Mindfulness requires intentional, non-judgmental focus of attention in the present moment. Meditation practice can increase your ability to focus and concentrate. In our distracted world, there is a lot of mindless activity.

Meditation is different from prayer in that it is not a supplication to the Divine or a Creator. Meditation is a means of transforming the mind. There are many ways to meditate. It's best to start with simple techniques for a short amount of time.

Staying in the moment is hard to do because the mind chatters and wanders off. "What's next? Where am I going? I need to do this and this and this." We're in a hurry to get done, and then what? There's always something else to do.

There is no there.

Become an Observer. Remain aware of your thoughts and actions without judgments about whether they are good, bad, or neutral. Step aside and just watch what's happening, like TV or a movie. Or, if you prefer to move out of your head and away from The Shitty Committee, try focusing on your senses of sight, smell, taste, and touch. The more you concentrate on your senses, the quieter your mind will become.

When thoughts arise it might occur to you to wonder where they come from. Where do they come from? It seems as if they arise from nowhere. You're following your breath and —Wham! you're planning dinner or worrying about finances. Emotions will arise. Don't attach to the story. There is no substance to your thoughts.

I was once instructed to meditate on thoughts. I investigated the nature of thought for two whole months. I never found one. There is nothing of substance there, but with our minds, we can make something an extremely big deal.

In the moment

What is happening as I write? The wind chimes are clanging because a hot wind is blowing. I am holding a lapis lazuli crystal heart in my left hand. Well, I was then. Now I'm on the computer typing a rough draft with the fan blowing. Everything changes from moment to moment.

For the first draft of this section, I decided to get off the computer and write by hand. It was 12:45 p.m. I looked down and realized I was still in my pajamas. "Ooops!" I thought, "I can take a shower, practice paying attention and then write about it as an example."

When I got in the shower and adjusted the temperature, I felt immense gratitude for the hot, running water. I smelled the shampoo, massaged my head, and enjoyed the physical sensations. The soap felt smooth on my skin. I thought about my friend Sue who makes the soap. I considered how connected we are to everything. Who made the shampoo? The bottles? The shower head? I know the plumber who installed the shower and the builder who built our house but who cut the wood and where did the trees grow?

Stepping out of the shower, the air felt cool. I stretched a bit, allowing myself some gentle activity. Lovingly I applied lotion to my skin that is always dry from our climate.

I became aware of grasping at concepts and striving to let go, yearning to feel the oneness of the universe.

Try this. No judgment.

Get in a comfortable position in a quiet place.

Take a deep breath. Count one on the inhalation.

Exhale.

Continue to the count of ten.

Rest.

Now.

Now.

Now.

When your mind wanders, bring it back.

Watch what happens.

Now take a deep breath and count one on the exhale.

Continue to the count of ten.

Rest.

Now.

Now.

Now.

How do you feel?

Meditation is a solitary process. Neuroscience has made it possible to determine the exact area of the brain that's affected by meditations. Years of research reveal that meditation produces positive changes that impact mental and physical health.

We all have patterns of reacting to the external world with our emotions, our minds, and our bodies. It helps to pay attention to what's happening from moment to moment. Your first gut emotional response to an external event is defined as an "amygdala hijack." Daniel Goleman coined this term. It's a hair-trigger response, usually in the form of an emotional outburst. This is because of neural pathways we've established in our brains. It's a form of emotional memory that isn't rational.

The neocortex of the brain is more reasonable, once it's accessed. Emotional intelligence is the ability to monitor your own emotions and label them appropriately. We can use this emotional information to learn how to emotionally regulate ourselves.

It gets easier. Many small moments of awareness will add up to big changes in your life. Notice small details. Breathe deeply. Slow down.

Often when you start to pay attention to your mind, it gets busier. Quieting the mind highlights the activity in there. Don't be concerned. The mind thinks. The trick is to let the thoughts go by, like watching the water move in a river. Don't attach to the thoughts. If you get distracted, and you will bring your mind back to center.

What happens when you become more aware?

What do you notice?

Try this simple mantra when you get hung up on judgments or mental chatter:

Let go.

Let be.

Emotional Mindfulness

Mindful awareness is basically paying attention to what's happening from moment to moment. We all have patterns of reacting to the external world with our emotions, our minds and our bodies.

Do you know what your patterns are?

Are you afraid of your feelings?

Do you know how to express them appropriately?

For example, what happens when your plans go awry? Whatever the reason - illness, traffic, finances - what is your first reaction? Anger? Disappointment? Why me? You make lemonade?

Describe these emotional patterns. Use your journal to track your responses to events during the day. The more often you pay attention, the more clear these patterns will become.

Over the course of our lifetime, we develop a litany of fears, resentments, and perhaps bitterness about the way things have gone. These negative emotions can build up over time and create a lot of difficulty as we age. No one wants to look back at a life filled with regret. Of course, there are regrets but it's what you tell yourself about the events that cause problems. Compassion and forgiveness are crucial in letting go of bitterness or regret.

Psychologists define forgiveness as a conscious, deliberate decision to release feelings of resentment or vengeance toward a person or group who has harmed you. This is regardless of whether or not they actually deserve your forgiveness. Forgiveness prevents negative emotional energy from building. The key is not who deserves forgiveness. The important factor is, again, in letting go.

Holding on to bitterness and resentment can poison you. It's been said that it's like "drinking poison hoping the other person will die." It's corrosive to your well-being. Pay attention to the stories you tell yourself. Forgiveness doesn't mean that you condone bad behavior. Neither does it mean that you reconcile with someone who has treated you badly. You don't forget what has happened to you, rather, you are making peace with the past and letting it go.

It's possible that you are your own worst enemy. Self-compassion is critical to moving forward and releasing negative emotions. If you let go and accept what already is, you won't change the past, you'll learn from it. Most likely you need to practice forgiving yourself.

What is your self-talk when you make a mistake? For example, do you say to yourself, "I'm a terrible, horrible, rotten person?" or some variation on the theme? As you journal about your emotional reactions, also record your self-talk. Pay attention.

If it becomes too painful, try writing in the 3rd person. It will help you act as your own "witness" and can help to remove critical judgments. Usually, we won't talk to a friend or loved one the way we talk to ourselves. You can step outside of yourself and look inside. If you write as an observer, "She is terrible — because she — —," does the energy or your perspective shift?

How can you love yourself more deeply?

What forms of kindness can you give yourself?

What would be the most loving thing you could do for yourself today?

PART FOUR: WALK ON A RAINBOW TRAIL

There is a way out of every dark mist, over a rainbow trail. ~Navaho Song

In Greco-Roman mythology, the rainbow was a path created by a messenger, Iris, between Earth and Heaven. A rainbow is truly a marvel of nature. It's a gift that encourages presence.

A rainbow doesn't actually exist in a particular location in the sky. Its position depends on your location and the position of the sun. The raindrops refract and reflect the sunlight but only the light from some raindrops reach your eyes.

The rainbow is there because of you.

How often do things in your life slip by without notice?

A guide is expected to understand the nature of the places she's guiding and to have an ability to answer questions about the places visited. I work really hard to navigate thick jungles of confusion. I use a machete to clear a path toward the light. I walk dark trails and find my way out of the mist.

Being committed to your spiritual life requires not only depth and compassion but also courage. Opening up to feelings, examining beliefs, and making changes is not easy. There are enormous rewards too. Feeling contentment, satisfaction and peace of mind are worth the effort it takes.

As it is on the spiral journey, one phase ends and another begins. Thank you for walking this far with me.

I offer this Metta Prayer:

> May you be at peace.
>
> May your heart remain open.
>
> May you awaken to the light of your own true nature.
>
> May you be healed.
>
> May you be a source of healing for all beings.

FINAL THOUGHTS

Journaling developed my self-awareness. Counseling helped me identify dysfunctional patterns. A twelve step program taught me how to admit my character defects to another and released me from shame. When I became willing to believe in a power greater than myself, my spiritual practices grew exponentially. Feminine nature-based community gave me support and improved my relationship with Earth, Gaia. There is a wealth of stories about goddesses and brave women available for study and inspiration.

As I started to age, I discovered that aging is treated like an illness no one wants to discuss. There are challenges and amazing opportunities for growth in maturity. I am becoming a Crone. I am always changing.

I hope your path feels a little more illuminated now. I've shared a bit about my grief, loss, addictions, frustrations, low self-esteem and body dysmorphia. Somewhere in the unseen, private life of a person is pain, sorrow, fear, happiness and joy. We run the gamut of feelings. We can heal our wounds. Perhaps now you're inspired to do some exploration on your own.

These are my words.

BIBLIOGRAPHY

Andrews, Ted, *Animal Speak*, Minnesota: Llewellyn Publication, 2011.

Bauers, Joanne Turney, T*he Art of Joyful Aging*, Washington, DC: Edgewood Publishing Company, 2009.

Cameron, Julia, with Bryan, Mark, *The Artists Way, A Spiritual Path to Higher Creativity,* New York: G. P. Putnam's Sons 1992.

Henes, Donna, *Queen of MySelf,* Monarch Press, 2012.

Nin, Anïas, *The Diary of Anïai Nin, Volumes I-VI, 1931-1966*, New York: Harcourt Brace Jovanovich, 1966-1976.

Noble, Vicki, *Motherpeace, A Way to the Goddess through Myth, Art and Myth, Art and Tarot,* San Francisco, Harper and Row, 1983.

Northrup, Christiane, *The Wisdom of Menopause*, Hay House Inc., 2021.

Progoff, Ira, *At a Journal Workshop*, New York: Dialogue House, 1975.

Rush, Anne Kent, *Moon, Moon*, New York: Random House, 1976.

Sahtouris, Elizabet, "Towards a Future Global Science," World Future Review, Dec. 2008.

Schaef, Anne Wilson; *Women's Reality,* HarperOne,1992.

Starhawk, *Dreaming the Dark, Magic, Sex & Politics*, Boston: Beacon Press, 1982.

Walker, Barbara G., *The Woman's Encyclopedia of Myths and Secrets*, San Francisco: Harper & Row Publishers, 1983.

ACKNOWLEDGMENTS

Thank you to my all my teachers and, specifically, those who taught me to write, think, ponder, and muse: Debra Marrs, Trista Hedren, and Lori Deschene. Thank you, Julie Daly, for reminding me to share my words. I appreciate all the friends I met online who supported my blogs and newsletters and those who invited me to write for them.

Blessings to Joanna Powell Colbert who has taught me so much about the Tarot and Walking the Sacred Wheel.

Great gratitude to my MoonSister, Kathryn Artinger Mensah, for exploring the mysteries with me. And huge hugs to my bestie in Sheridan, Kathleen Lundberg, who encourages me in all ways.

My brilliant sister, Joni Currier, graciously agreed to proofread my text. Thank you for always being a fan of my writing.

Shout out to my husband, Gary Martin, who has managed to cope with my ups and downs throughout the years and continues to support my many creative efforts.

And finally, to my dad, Bill Bauers, who liked to write too. I stole your publishing name.

AUTHOR'S BIO

C. Loran Hills is a retired counselor, social worker, and community organizer. She spent most of her adulthood searching for answers to the deeper questions of life. Through hard work and years of exploration, she has some answers of her own.

She loves nature, hiking, camping, photography, and travel around the world. She's a creative multipotentialite, always experimenting with new things.

She lives with her husband in Wyoming, along with two miniature Schnauzers, four cats and seven chickens. Her adult daughters flew the nest and she misses them all the time.